WE ARE CHILDREN OF THE EVOLUTION

WRITTEN BY

ANDREW STEED

1

COPYRIGHT

DEDICATION

This book is dedicated to my granddaughter Múirin, whose name means "Born of the Sea." It was birthed from a vision that I received in the land of wood and water — Jamaica, fuelled by a voyage on the Caribbean Sea. May you live a long, joyful, and gracious life Múirin and may those that came before you stand together so that all sentient beings that come behind you are able to celebrate the beauty, love, truth, freedom, and Sovereignty of the worlds in all of their glory!

ACKNOWLEDGEMENTS

I would like to share my heartfelt gratitude for my partner Joyce who walks beside me in this world. Thank you, Joyce, for your love, generosity of spirit and self-sacrifice in supporting me and my medicine walk on the planet. You are an extraordinary woman whose work often goes unseen yet makes such a difference in my life and in so many lives of other beings on the planet. I appreciate you supporting the work in the ethers when your bodies exclude you from traveling. Every step of the way I feel you and having you with me in spirit and in person gives me extra strength to be a medicine way, I love you. Thank you for your insights and clarity in being a midwife for the birthing of this book!

A huge thank you to Spirit for guiding me to see myself more clearly. Thank you to the ancestors and all of the unseen beings who come again and again to celebrate life, death-rebirth in such magical ways.

A book takes a village to support its composition. Jenna Redhawk, thank you for diligently editing and formatting my words. You are a star! I appreciate how quickly you responded to bringing this work to fruition and for climbing readily on the boat to be part of this journey.

Great gratitude to Louise Robb for being a sounding board, for your attention to detail and for being willing to help raise the sail in seeing this work find its way into the world.

Jayde Hilliard, you are amazing! Thank you for your flexibility and phenomenal talent. I had a clear vision of what the front cover of the book looked like and you were able to breathe life into that vision. Thank you for agreeing to take this on in your busy season. You exceeded all my hopes for what the final design would look like.

My Mum and Dad, Elizabeth Grace Steed and Anthony John Robert Steed, I am eternally grateful for your love and support of my wandering outside the lines of convention. Having you there as a sounding board is a true gift.

To all of my Ancestors and Guides who stand with me, thank you. To the Mitchell Clan whose lands called to me and have brought me back to a heart home in the Kingdom of Fife, thank you for having my back!

Thanks, Tanaaz Chubb, for readily agreeing to allow me to put your words from your vision into the book and for sharing your light with the world.

Doron Alon, I am grateful you chose to come on pilgrimage with me. You have been a rock in helping with all of my books, negotiating the publishing process is challenging for a non- tech person like myself, your knowledge and support are invaluable.

A huge thank you to Joey Stuart for inviting me to send him the audio files for editing. I so appreciate my extended family that you are a part of now, Joey, thanks to Doron and Kristin Pamperin.

Steph Brown, I really appreciate your collaboration with all of the artists that have worked on the cover designs for my books. Thank you for adding an extra sprinkling of magic to complete the designs.

Thank you, Margaret Greer, for your selflessness in helping me connect with my ancestral roots.

Thank you, Pat Beck, for your friendship, love, and trust. Wandering between the worlds with you is always magical.

Thank you, Michael Fenster and Jenn Fenster, for your constant support and for being part of so many magical journeys with Joyce and I. Your generosity in inviting us to sail on the High Seas of the Caribbean sparked a light towards illuminating an evolutionary pathway, for that, I am eternally grateful.

Thank you, Mark and Bobby, for sailing us to the edge of the world.

Thank you, Jackie Lewis and all of the staff at Jackie's on the Reef — Gwen, Vanetta, Nick, Oshane, Overton, Sabina, Dr. Scott, Stephanie, and all of those who have been part of the journey in serving those who have been blessed to wander your way.

Thank you, Roberta Reeves, for sharing my name with Jackie and paving the way for my arrival on the reef.

Thank you to all of those who have travelled to the reef with me over the last few years, Joyce, Pat, Margaret, Megan, Tara, Jeff, Cindy, Kay, Janis, Jan, Mike, Racheal, Nikki, Jenn, Mike, Aylish, Bob, Jean and Karen.

Thank you to the 250 plus people who sent in their prayers and lit candles and fires to join us in the ethers of the Full Moon Birthing Fire — Your connection magnifies the magic.

Thank you, Mitchell Clute, for agreeing so readily to write the foreword and for helping share the importance for waking up through all that you do with Sounds True and to Sandra Ingerman for connecting me with Mitchell and the Sounds True team.

I am so grateful for all of the support from so many beings along this trail — Mulina and Emerson, Jan and Mike, Derek and Alison, Izzie and Denis, Janis and Cristiano, Howard and Elsa, Leslie, and Andrew and the countless souls whose paths have met mine and helped shape me in the worlds.

WRITING DISCLAIMER

I have always had a fascination with language. I love how in the film, *Christopher Robin,* Pooh asks Christopher, "A fish in the sea?" when referring to what he was talking about — "efficiency."

As a child I painted outside of the lines of convention; as an adult, I have danced to the beat of my own drum. As a writer, I bring my life experiences of living in three different countries, England, USA, and Scotland to the table. For the purists, you will find what you consider "mistakes" in spelling, grammar, and capitalization as I weave a hybrid language from my time spent in these lands. On paper, we may speak the same language, yet in reality, some of our words have completely different meanings, spellings, and are not recognised as we cross borders and Oceans!

Add to this my own propensity for making up or taking on new words. As a wise elder in the First Nations of the USA medicine way once shared with me, "Why would you place *tension* in the word intention when you could let it flow by setting an *intending*?" It made sense to me so I now have *intendings*!

I have also chosen to use the term *history* though, in reality, it ought to read *ourstory* for alongside *history* there is *herstory* to consider.

For those who have chosen the audiobook, you will also notice that my pronunciation shows that I have lived on both sides of the Atlantic as I sometimes use Caribbean while also saying Caribbean.

So yes, I honour the purists and put my hand up to admit that my writing has quirks that mirror my own colourful personality and I ask that you join me on the voyage by exploring the content. My hope is that whichever spelling I have chosen to use, the heart of the story speaks to your soul and leads us to dance side by side on a pathway to evolution!

FOREWORD

We live in a world of magic, a world woven by spirit, ripe with signs and portents. The energies of the rocks and water, the earth and sky, the moon and stars, all of these are offered to us. It is our birthright as human beings to participate fully in this world—not merely the world the eye can see and the mind can comprehend, but an entire universe of meaning and possibility, inside us and outside us.

It's not just for our own healing that the time has come to remember what it means to be fully alive and to claim the full range of our human being. We have only to look at the deep wounds our earth has suffered through our lack of care, at the frayed connections within our human families, to understand why it is vital now for each of us to evolve into deeper connection—with ourselves, with our beloved ones, with all the beings on this earth journey with us, with all the powers and potencies available to us through the endless generosity of life.

As a species, we have learned much from our long foray into civilization. We've built great cities, composed symphonies, carved our knowledge in the stones of our temples and printed it in the pages of our books. We've discovered technologies that connect us, medicines that heal us; we have harnessed powers that would seem magic to our ancestors. But what we have forgotten is of much greater worth than all the discoveries of mind. What we have forgotten is our song—the human song, unique as a fingerprint, that each of us is born to express, and the one song of spirit that informs and enlivens this whole precious world.

That is why *Children of the Evolution* is such a timely and important offering. Andrew Steed is a weaver of words and a weaver of worlds, one who understands the deep magic of life. Such a tapestry of words is always a beautiful gift, but in the times we are traveling now it is also a necessary one. In this book, Andrew braids together the magic of his own story with the vaster story of what it means to be human—

fully alive, fully open to the call of spirit—and in sharing this most personal of narratives, he shows how each of us can heed the deepest calling in our hearts and follow a path to wholeness.

Andrew is one who hears the song of Amrun, the spirit song that sings us into being and carries our medicine into the world. He hears the song; he sings it; he lives it. It is no small thing simply to be who we are, to trust the soul and the body life has given us, and to sing our song in the world. He is a guide to be trusted; he has walked the path through all its trials and all its miracles.

I had the pleasure of reading Andrew's manuscript as I travelled the highlands of Peru. I carried it with me along ancient footpaths as I walked among the *Apus*, the sacred mountains of that land. At every turn, I was welcomed by the Quechua-speaking natives of those high and wild places. When we shared pisco, they always offered the first draught of liquor to our mother Pachamama. When we shared coca, before taking any for themselves they offered a *kintu*—three unblemished leaves gathered together and enlivened with breath and prayer—to the mountains and the beings of the land. They understood the living world of spirit that surrounds and supports us, and made their offerings to bring all things into balance through *ayni*, the sacred reciprocity and gratitude at the heart of the Andean worldview.

I feel this same spirit of *ayni* in Andrew's words. He is deeply grounded in the tales and traditions of the Celtic lands, a masterful storyteller and maker of meaning. But the message he shares here goes beyond any one place or one tradition. All the shamanic paths, the deep wisdom paths grounded in honoring the earth and in the wisdom of our own hearts and bodies, share the same commitment to transforming us so we can be vessels of spirit—fully alive, fully ourselves, yet fully engaged in the magic of life for the benefit of all beings.

Maybe you have heard this song of creation welling up inside you, quietly, as you sit beneath the stars or walk a forest path or gaze at a beloved one. Maybe you are already following it into the mystery. When we grow empty, the world can sing its song through us. When we are a hollow bone, the melody arises naturally within us. When we trust, miracles happen—simple as the moon rising or the clouds moving in the sky.

May the magic in this book light a fire in your heart so that you discover the deep magic of your own life, your own journey. May you sing your spirit song in everything you do, with every step you take. May your song bring you home.

Mitchell Clute
Host, The Shamanic Path
Senior Producer, Sounds True
The Guy You Asked to Write the Foreword

CHAPTER 1: EXTINCTION OR EVOLUTION? THE CHOICE IS OURS!

Do I have a story for you! A tale that has changed how I see the world and my hope is that you will be called to stay with me for the whole journey through these writings, for with it, I believe it will help change your world, my world, and all of our worlds for the better. It will require opening your heart to the possibility of evolution and a willingness to bring that heart of yours to the challenges that lay ahead.

I will take you on the high seas, where on a boat ride off the coast of Jamaica I was brought face to face with death. It was in the eye of the storm that a vision of redemption for humanity and all beings on planet Earth was clearly shown to me. Here within this tale lies a solution and a pathway to the evolution of our species and all beings seen and unseen.

Before I get to the main meal, the flesh that drives the story, I must first lay out some of the bones so that the story has context. For those who are eager to board the boat and raise the sail and cannot wait to catch the wind, I advocate patience, raise the anchor and breathe in the adventure of this journey. Of course, you can always jump ahead and my hope is that you will read all of the pieces laid out here. For some, this may be old news, to others it will be a revelation, and for many of the general populace, there are challenging concepts that patterned brains may try to reject. To those who would typically scoff at the ideas presented here, I invite you to look into the world outside of the bubble in which most of us have sequestered ourselves in and ask — is the world in chaos right now? Do you see, feel, hear the pain, hopelessness, anger, fear that pervades so many aspects of life on planet Earth?

If like me your answer is yes, is there a curiosity within you to discover ways to alleviate the suffering? Is there a desire to live life vibrantly and to see others thrive rather than desperately survive on the planet?

If so, I am excited to share this pathway to change. For those who have read some of my other books, or worked with others who speak a similar language to me here, forgive any repetition in the set up and please do not discard this work until you have sailed on the Caribbean Sea with me, returned to the port, and sat by the 13-hour full moon birthing fire that was lit in celebration of all life. For in so doing I hope it will ignite a fire in your belly, a fire in your head so that you will join me and those like me in bringing these fires to unite together in our hearts. A collective flame that has the potential to re-dream the worlds!

SIR DAVID ATTENBOROUGH

Sir David Attenborough is considered a national treasure in the British Isles. He is a natural historian and pioneer of connecting people to animal and plant life on Earth through his collaborative work with the BBC's natural history programmes including *The Life Collection Series.*

When Attenborough speaks of the imminent collapse of civilizations through climate change, it is time for the world to listen. He advocates that the leaders of the world must lead, for the destruction of many species, regions, and countries is coming ever the closer, as climate change is running faster than we are.

He has publicly stated that if we don't take action, the collapse of our civilizations and the extinction of much of the natural world is on the horizon.

There is a movement on the planet whereby humans are asking other humans to "wake up." I believe that as Attenborough challenges humans to take responsibility, the idea of "waking up" begins at an individual level. If I fail to "wake up" then I will be one of the sleepwalkers that, on our current course, follow the masses like lemmings over the cliff. This drop, however, leads to extinction!

A HARSH TRUTH

As Attenborough correctly surmises, human beings have caused one almighty problem with an ever increasing population growth and our craving to harness the planet to our will. We have decimated the oceans, driven so many other species to the brink of extinction, raped the land and for time immemorial, we have waged war on each other. Many leaders have placed their personal power, greed, and a thirst for dominion over all other beings, including other humans, and the Earth above the welfare of all.

It is a harsh truth that many do not want to face. It is easier to live in a bubble and hide from the reality of our collective actions through tribalism in sports, computer games, alcohol, sex, consumerism, creating avatars of ourselves on social media, and a host of other pursuits that lead us to bury our heads in the sand.

SOLUTION

As much as we are the problem, I also have held the light of hope in my heart that we are also the solution. For many years now I have taught from a place of hope; I am now heartened to share that I can now teach from a place of knowing. What transpired in Jamaica has gifted me with a flame of knowledge that we can change the tide of destruction. Will we? That, dear reader, depends on you and many like you. It won't be a saviour who comes to Earth and fixes the mess that us humans have co-created. It will be the lay folk and the great news is we have the numbers to do it if we are willing. It will take huge work and a concentrated effort and what I saw is it is absolutely possible!

FROM THE MOUTH OF BABES

It is not only renowned scholars like Sir David who are lighting a torch for change. How wonderful it is to see our youth take an active role in calling for change. Leading the charge is 16-year-old Greta Thunberg from Sweden whose voice is being heard at the highest levels of government. She has spoken eloquently and bluntly to world leaders at the World Economic Forum in Geneva. Her matter of fact statements has challenged the authorities as she has urged them to "panic" stating, "Our house is on fire!" She cites the Intergovernmental Panel on Climate Change's finding that we are less than 11 years away from not being able to undo our mistakes. Her words ring true to me when she states, "All political movements in their present forms have failed and the media has failed to create broad public awareness."

Yet Greta holds hope in her heart. I agree with her when she informs world leaders that homo sapiens have not failed yet. We indeed hold the key to solving the most complex challenge that our race has ever met, right now we have the whole world in our hands. The question is whether we are willing to place the whole world in our hearts?

Greta's words have lit a torch within communities around the world; however, let's work with the knowledge that extinction is on the horizon to flame the fires of hope rather than destruction. I understand that the realization that climate change could bring devastation to many species on the planet is scary. It will invoke a reaction. Some may stick their heads further in the sand in denial, some may get angry and protest, some may become angry at those who have shared the information and retaliate by blaming the protestors. When fear raises its head it is easy to get swept up in the wildfire of chaos. It is easy to get stuck in the blame game and create further threads that tether us to the problem. It is going to take discernment and wisdom to bring all of this to our own doorstep and to look at our carbon footprints, our thoughts and actions that are either reacting to the problems or responding to being an active part of the solution.

FROM HOPE TO KNOWING

What changed in me to be able to replace hope with a comprehensive knowing is an incredible story of many parts that unfolded in Jamaica. I had gathered there with a group to lead a retreat to celebrate all life in February 2019.

What I will outline through these writings is a way to support each of us in participating in the evolution of humankind and all of our relations, a vision to guide us in re-dreaming the worlds. Each of us has the capacity to choose to play as big or small a role in rebirthing ourselves into a new way of being. The question is — are you open minded and open hearted enough to grasp the opportunity with both hands or will you dismiss these writings as pure fancy, a fairy-tale that is too fearful to behold?

LEADERS

Whose hands are we placing the power of leadership in? Many world leaders, the politicians, and big business conglomerates that drive the decisions on which our world is based have operated from a place of greed and fear. Of course, it is important for those in a place of power in world governments to step forward and activate major change for the benefit of the planet. However, I believe handing the problem to these people solely and trusting them now to be the main driving force to revolutionise the way we operate in relationship to all life is foolhardy and disempowering to the collective.

If we think our individual role in the evolution of our species does not matter, we will perpetuate the problem. Quite simply, we will demonstrate an old pattern of doing the same thing the same way and expecting a different result. This, as I am sure you are aware, is the definition of insanity.

Each of us has the capacity to lead and follow. For lay people like myself, we have historically given our power away to the mysterious "they." "They," say this. "They," say that. We adopt an "I can't" attitude as we question — what difference will my actions make? We play small a great deal in life — why?

I think we have been programmed to do so. The machine of society has dictated a way for us to conform, to fit into the lines of convention. When someone strays they are made to feel an outcast. It is an interesting aspect of human existence, this desperate need to fit in that comes into play so early in our lives through the institutions that are part and parcel of our world.

DREAMERS

Those of us who are placed into the category of dreamers, the creative types that paint outside of the lines are often seen as being way out there — touched, affected, weirdos — people to be mistrusted because they buck the trends of normality. Yet, if we dare to look beyond the chains that have bound us to the brink of destruction, perhaps there is a method within the perceived madness that may just provide the planet with a way to breathe, a way to reinvent itself. Are you ready and willing to be part of a (r)evolution into evolution? To enter the fray in a very different way as we fight a war from a place of love rather than hatred, from joy rather than fear, from our hearts rather than our heads? For make no mistake, we are at war; I believe that this is for us human beings, a war to end all wars, a war that has two possible outcomes — extinction or evolution. Whichever side we take homo sapiens will play a pivotal and either a short term or long term role in relationship with planet Earth!

So I ask you which path will you choose? Will you stay entrenched in the old ways of war or will you join those who are remembering, reweaving, and rebirthing a new world? Will you choose to fight against a system that you may feel has let us down, or will you choose to stand with those who are looking to be the vibration of change and become part of the solution?

WAR

When I was a child I was told that the war was over, that my grandparents fought in a war to end all wars. How wonderful it was to live in peacetime. Yet as a very young boy I witnessed separation and attacks on other children and adults within my own hometown of Bury St. Edmunds in Suffolk, England. These hometown wars were fought because of religious differences, ethnicity, sexuality, a division in the perceived value of men over women, of Caucasians over all other races and of humankind over the Earth and all of the other life forms that inhabit the planet.

Though we were not at war in a conventional sense, the fighting and feuding between families, housing estates, schools, neighbouring towns, and the numerous fashion and musical trends from mods, rockers, skinheads, punks, soul boys etc. kept the merry-go-round of war at its parasitical best.

My parents tuned into the news every night and footage of bombings and gunfire from Beirut to sporadic IRA attacks were in our living room on a daily basis. As one decade turned into another, wars have raged on. As a keen reader of historical fiction set in the British Isles, writers such as Sharon Penman, Bernard Cornwall, and Ken Follett paint a tapestry of bloodshed through the ages from Neolithic Stonehenge through to modern day.

In my own life, I narrowly missed being aboard a train that was blown up by bandits in Peru, I was held hostage in India, and dove for cover as a drunken man shot bullets from a handgun in a shady side street that I had inadvertently wandered down in the city of Puno, also in Peru.

In my early twenties, I stood beside a friend who was stabbed in the small village of Thurston near Bury St. Edmunds, who a week later had his ear ripped off as a beer glass was rammed into his face. And then a few years later I witnessed another friend being stabbed in the Grapes pub also in Bury St. Edmunds. I was chased through Carnaby Street in London by skinheads who caught up with me and stuck their boots in as I lay helpless on the pavement. This attack was in broad daylight and witnessed by a bunch of people who looked on in fear.

Fortunately, I have avoided serious injuries from assaults and skirmishes in my life including being mugged in the early hours in downtown Lima, Peru. The long and the short of it — surviving adolescence and making it through my twenties into my thirties and beyond seems quite a feat when I look back through the montage of battles that I went through! All apparently in peacetime and my experiences are not untypical for homo sapiens throughout the world, with many experiencing far worse through rape, murder, torture, and the modern day slave trade.

From the primary school playground to the board room bullying and harassment make a mockery of the teachings "sticks and stones may break your bones but names will never hurt." The stinging taunts of smear campaigns using the spoken and written word cut into the self-esteem of the populace like knives. Alongside our tongues — bottles, knives, guns, and bombs are as prevalent in today's world as they have been in each and every age where weapons of destruction have been used.

A BLEAK PICTURE

Sex trafficking, the slave trade, and the profits from the war industry are as rife today as at any time in our planet's history. Our world is caked in the blood of our ancestors and it doesn't stop there. With so much fear, anger, abuse, jealousy, betrayal, pain, suffering, loneliness, grief, fatigue, hopelessness, despair, depression, disease, unworthiness, manipulation, greed, self-absorption, anxiety, sorrow, and possession as part of our world's history, both past and present, the patterns created have left a harsh trail of tangled knots and blocked energy that is screaming throughout the planet in myriad ways.

It is a bleak picture and on the surface, it looks like we are well and truly up sh-t creek without a paddle! I recently walked through the city of Edinburgh looking at the swarms of people hustling and bustling in the safety of their bubbles and wondered how the clarity of the message that I received in Jamaica can be imparted to the masses.

It would be easy to drown in the tide of despair witnessing the lines at McDonald's which are always full, plastic food for a plastic age. The craving of our quick fix fast food approach in the Western World, an insatiable appetite that cannot be sated by empty foods and goods designed to break. The machine of consumerism continues to rape the Earth's resources, as people gorge on inauthenticity in a desperate need to fill an unquenchable void within them. In the face of such alarming odds, it is easy to buy into the hopelessness of it all. The old adage of p-ssing in the wind comes to mind!

Each of us leaves a carbon footprint on the Earth. I certainly do and it is my responsibility to take ownership of my actions and take active steps to reduce it. It is a responsibility that we are all being asked to face. Living in the twenty-first century with all of our modern conveniences in the Western World is both a blessing and a challenge. In 1987, when I was in India, I spent some time living in a house with some Indian students whereby each day we would walk to a well and carry buckets of water home to bathe and cook; we had no electricity so we made fires to cook and relied on candles at night time. It gave me a deep appreciation for the stove, the fridge, and the tap/spigot that I have in my home. I wonder how many of us have become over-reliant on technology? Like many, I run a business that is dependent on the internet, electricity, travel, and a host of emissions that reduce the space and quality of life for the natural world.

I will address this more anon, and for now, I would like to focus on shifting our mindset from hopelessness, beyond the horizon of hope, into knowing that — *we can.*

I fully understand the journey to evolution is at such odds to what we have accepted to be the norm in most cultures currently living on the planet.

To say the least, the rebirthing of the worlds appears overwhelming.

YES, I CAN — YES, WE CAN

My beautiful partner Joyce reminded me recently to stop and breathe when the darkness seems so thick and I feel like I am being swept up in the chaos of it all. A simple remedy of closing my eyes, putting my hand on my heart and stating with the belief of feeling "Yes, I can!" is a ten-second game changer! As each of us makes a difference and steps out of hopelessness into believing we can, we add our "yes I can" to a global "yes we can!"

As my mind plays tricks of old patterns whereby I question whether the vision I have received will be mocked and dismissed, I face the illusion of this fear. As threads of failure gnaw into my mind teasing me that the masses will ridicule what they do not understand in favour of past patterns that don't work anymore, I step through the fear and activate my choice of how I will respond in each and every moment. In the words of young Greta, "We all have a choice. We can create transformational action that will safeguard the living conditions for future generations. Or we can continue with our business as usual and fail!"

COURAGE TO SPEAK UP

It takes courage to speak our truth, especially when it is outside of conventional thinking. By doing so we risk rejection. I know this first hand for I have experienced the rejection of our species many times in my life. Interestingly, from a mainstream society who advocates "thinking outside of the box" yet attack ideas that threaten they open their boxes to a new way of being. The security blanket, however, frayed and moth-eaten, seems to give comfort and if people can wrap it ever more tightly around them perhaps they can shut out the light as they wallow in the darkness of despair.

Perhaps their hope is that if they turn off the light then it will all go away, perhaps the imminent destruction of the planet is just a bad nightmare that we will all awaken from refreshed and invigorated. This idea of whatever seems to be easier is always more difficult and whatever seems to be more difficult is ultimately easier is a hard pill to swallow in the quick fix age. Why? Well, it means taking responsibility. It means facing our own shadows, meeting ourselves where we are at and being willing to change direction. It means being in relationship with ourselves in a healthy way so we can be in healthy relationships with all other beings. For the masses who have been content hiding in their heads and disappearing from being present with themselves and others, it is a major shift. Yet, if we are going to step away from the definition of insanity and do things in a different way to get a different result, only a major shift will do it!

HOPE PREVAILS

In the swirling seas of chaos — hope prevails. It has certainly fed my fire for many years now and after my recent experiences in Jamaica, I have a new satellite to guide me. I believe fervently that we can win this war and I am willing to devote my life to the cause. The great news is the war that I am embroiled in looks and feels very different than conventional war. It is centred on transmutation from sorrow to joy so that we can activate peace. A war without bloodshed, a war that celebrates life, death, and rebirth whereby instead of killing the beings we work to liberate them. A war that offers a chance for all beings to win!

WAR TO RAW

Perhaps the word *war* itself is outdated. I have used it here as a reference point so that people can understand the desperate times that face us. As I sat wondering how to rename a word that has such an aggressive nature associated with it I was reminded from Spirit that we are looking to turn things around, to be willing to look at life in a different way. It was then that I looked into the mirror of desire as young Harry Potter did. In so doing it reminded me of how J.K. Rowling had taken the word *desire* and flipped it into *erised*. I did the same with *war* to spell *raw*. One meaning of raw is fresh and looking at the world through fresh eyes is certainly being called for. As I played with this acronym three definitions came flowing through — *Reweaving a way, Rebirthing a way, Remembering a way* — I then burst out laughing as I roared "RAW" on the wind!

Again I ask you, will you stay entrenched in the old ways of war or will you open your heart and raw with me?

PARADIGM SHIFT

As I sat talking to a Mac specialist in the Apple store on Princes Street in Edinburgh I spoke of Jamaica and the life-changing events that took place there. The technician who was helping me with a fault on my computer perked up as I shared a glimpse of what happened there. I didn't go into details. I shared only that unless we are willing to look beyond our current methods for being human on the planet — we face extinction. I was transparent in voicing that many people may think I am fruit loop because my ideas are outside of their normal parameters for how the world works. I offered him a light of hope as I spoke with an assurance that we can activate change, that in Jamaica I had received information that illuminates a pathway to this change.

This short conversation spoke to the man, perhaps it was the realisation that it is the lay people of the world who will win this newly named *raw* by wrestling control away from the current leaders of our world. That it isn't one or two people that will lead us into the evolution, that it is the everyday folk, the hidden heroes whose hearts joined together can activate change. He asked when this book will be out as he was keen to read it. He shared from his perspective that major change happens with ideas that the populace initially ridicule, that the pioneers of change have always offered revolutionary ideas that lead to paradigm shifts. I am sure that the idea that the world was not in fact flat was once met with ridicule!

When I spoke about the collective coming together and a notion of bringing enough souls on board whereby a point of critical mass would be reached, it made absolute sense to him. He totally got that it is possible to open spaces within our bodies for the evolution of humankind to take place. He accepted totally the notion that those who did not see the vision would be swept up in the rebirthing of the world by those who were actively a part of the change.

NEW LEADERS

The new leaders of our world will look different than those of the past. I believe it will be the visionaries who are able to read the tapestry of this magical world and interpret it for those who are thirsty for change to understand and get wholeheartedly behind. The world is full of magic, yet mainstream society has developed a fear of this term and relegated those who believe in it to the oddballs who are often labelled as dangerous to the status quo. The more I have followed my heart and opened myself to the magic that is inherent both within the world and within my own bodies, the spiritual, mental, and physical aspects of myself, the more magic that presents itself to me!

Does this new leadership preclude current leaders? Not at all, the beauty of this pathway to evolution is that each of us gets to choose how big or small a part we play in it. Obviously the bigger the investment the greater the chance we have in winning this *raw*.

LESS THAN 11 YEARS

Sir David Attenborough doesn't give a timeline for the catastrophic events that he predicts are on our horizons without drastic change, whereas the Intergovernmental Panel on Climate Change, as I have stated before, gives us less than 11 years.

I recently flew into Washington Dulles in early February and it was 75 degrees Fahrenheit/23 Celsius and within a few days, it was freezing, sleeting, and snowing. It doesn't take a rocket scientist to know that the seasons are out of alignment. Placing a number on our challenge was quite the comfort and awakening for me. I have known for a long time that the lightest light is rising to meet the darkest dark that is sweeping across the planet. I have spoken often of a time when we will meet critical mass. I have always felt that this would be in my lifetime as I truly believe it is why I came to the planet, why many of us came to the planet at this moment in time. We are the ones who we have been waiting for and now is our moment to shine!

The naming of a number brings the horizon into perspective. It is a comfort because it has fueled the confirmation of this knowing that I have had inside of me, that the work that I have been diligently stirring for the highest good of all beings over the years has been in preparation for this moment.

It is an awakening for me because of a saying that has been with me in my teachings for many years now, a saying that makes sense in a very new way. The saying is, "Is there a horizon beyond the horizon?"

Try getting to the horizon, it always shifts. Yet a new horizon, one of fewer than 11 years has been put forward and in Jamaica, I was shown a glimpse of the horizon beyond the horizon. We are sailing into extinction or evolution and whichever horizon we choose to navigate our way toward, will be the key to the rebirthing of the planet for all beings.

This is a deeper awakening within me for this finish and starting line, this line of life, death, and rebirth is now tangible and it is both closer and further away from us all.

CLOSER AND FURTHER

Why closer and further? Simply stated, 11 years is a drop in the ocean in the parameters of the Earth's story. In fact, it is more of a drop within a drop! However, if you close your eyes and picture yourself 11 years ago and then take a wander through all that has transpired in your life from that period to current day, you may as I do see that you have lived lifetimes within lifetimes in these 11 years. One thing to understand here is that time is an illusion, sometimes it appears to stretch out and at other times it swings rapidly by. We certainly have a huge task ahead of us and if we work diligently towards an evolutionary horizon and enough people get aboard the boat, then I know we can achieve it!

CHAPTER 2: SPACE, DEATH, AND THE TAPESTRY OF LIFE

THE LYMPHATIC SYSTEM

On the way to the Baltimore and Washington International airport, to board a flight to Montego Bay in February 2019, my good friend Pat Beck posed an interesting question to me. It came out of the blue and provided a platform for what was to unfold on the reef of the Caribbean Sea.

She asked about the lymphatic gland in relationship to the Earth. She was curious about how the Earth excretes the pollutants that contaminate her body.

Those familiar with Spirit songs will probably know the refrain, "Earth my body, water my blood, air my breath, and fire my spirit." She was curious to which element the lymphatic gland equated to in relationship with the Earth. My initial response was to ask my partner Joyce for she is incredible with relating the meaning of body parts in relationship to our lives.

However, as I sat there pondering the question I realised I knew exactly what the relationship of the lymphatic gland is with the Earth and the elements.

I related that it was all of them and sometimes a mix of them. The forest fires, volcanic eruptions, tsunamis, tornadoes, earthquakes, floods all of these so-called natural disasters are ways for the Earth to cleanse and heal.

What happened next was many small signs that fed into a much bigger picture. These signs are part of the tapestry of life.

TAPESTRY

Many people rush through life trying to get wherever they think they need to go. Small signs drift across our pathways each and every day. We may name them coincidences or oddities, we may dismiss them, fail to register them and in time tune them out. The world around us is always speaking and when we listen we realise that there is no such thing as a coincidence.

These signs are threads of the tapestry and as we open and listen to them they amplify, more come through and a magical realm begins to take shape before us. I have found that it takes time and patience and for those that follow the threads the tapestry becomes easier to read.

AN EXAMPLE OF FOLLOWING A THREAD

On the summit of Slieve na Calliagh, also known as the Hill of the Hag, at Loughcrew in Co. Meath, Ireland, the beginnings of a magical story stirred. It was the summer of 2014, I had climbed out of an ancient burial chamber and had perched myself close to the Hags Seat taking in the magnificent views that sweep far and wide across the landscape.

As I breathed in the glory of a day filled with electric blue skies and bright sunshine I felt a pair of bright eyes smiling upon me. They belonged to a ruddy-faced red-headed giant of a man who introduced himself as a local blacksmith. We hit it off immediately, we shared a wonderful camaraderie in that brief exchange, so much so that it felt like we had been friends for years. Before we parted he shared that he had a gift for me.

"Now I'm sure you know the Hill of Tara," he beamed. "But would you be knowing the Faerie Tree by the grove of trees that leads into the Faerie Wood?"

"I absolutely do," I replied. "I always gather the pilgrims under the hawthorn tree and share stories before heading into that wood." The wood in question is my favourite haunt on Tara. The moss licked trees sing of a time between time, a place where the Fae fly freely, even if you were ne'er to set your eyes upon them, a vivid imagination would paint pictures of the wee folk peeking from behind every tree.

"Those woods are full of the Fae!" I exclaimed.

"Indeed they are!" He giggled. "Those woods are not only my favourite place to wander, they are my children's favourite. We collected acorns this year and now have many young saplings sprouting up. I have two trees for you to take home with you."

As I had flown to Ireland I was not in a position to take them with me then and there. My new found friend whose name was Tom assured me that he would look after them until a time came when I was able to pick them up.

The beauty of this encounter is that we stayed in touch. A year after meeting I moved to the Kingdom of Fife which I later found out was an ancestral seat of power for my family, thanks to the generosity of my second cousin Margaret Greer who traced my mother's lineage for me. It was such a heartfelt gesture as this side of my family is totally unrelated to hers. She discovered that all of my ancestors from my mother's line reaching as far back as 1702 were all, up to and including my mother, born in the Kingdom of Fife. I literally had come home!

Another year passed and I took my car over on the ferry from Cairnryan to Belfast and drove down to meet Tom on the Hill of Tara to collect the trees. For those of you who are familiar with the story of Tara Hill, you will know that according to tradition it is the seat of the High King of Ireland. It is said that Tara was the capital and just like it is said all roads led to Rome, in Ireland, all roads led to Tara!

A magical story requires patience and an ability to look and decipher the clues that the Universe provides for us. As we do it reveals a much bigger picture.

In the "Celtic" stories the oak tree is known as the King of Trees. I was receiving them from a man whose full name is Tom King. The meaning of the name Tom is twin. My hope is to plant them in the village of my Grandmother's birth, Kemback. I was recently told by the daughter of the owner of the estate at Kemback Hall that in the Norse tradition one of the meanings of Kemback is "Field of the King."

The county of Fife is commonly referred to as the Kingdom of Fife which has its roots in the Pictish Kingdom of Fib.

One other important factor in the equation here is Tara is also known as the place of Sovereignty and the animal totem associated with the "Celtic" goddess Sovereignty is the horse. Another name for a horse is steed.

With all of this information gathered we have an intriguing thread that brought a blacksmith and wordsmith onto a hill named for a goddess, the Cailleach, and they struck a fire of friendship that has resulted in the twin king gifting twin kings from seeds gathered at the seat of the High King that will be planted in the Kingdom of Fife in the Field of the King by the one who carries the name of the goddess. A bringing together of divine masculine and feminine energy!

Interestingly, the number five is the number that connects to Sovereignty in the "Celtic" tradition.

Where the earth, air, fire, and water meet in the centre, where our east, south, west, and north meet in our centre. As the trees find a permanent home this year, it will be five years since their birth in which they have been lovingly tended by five people, Tom King and his two children and by myself and my partner Joyce. What a right royal story has been stirred!

FIVE YEARS

I arrived in Jamaica to lead a retreat and light a fire in February 2019, five years to the day that I had begun the work on the reef. It was February 14, 2014, that the full moon arose in the sky at 11.52pm in Scotland. Although the full moon was February 19th in 2019, the first part of the retreat was to take place on February 14th.

I remember the full moon of 2014 well for we did not see the moon that night. I gathered with two friends under a snow-laden sky and lit a fire of intending. As the flames licked the air the snow hung from the trees and drenched us. Energetically we were rainbows in the fire and water that was created that night.

At the same time our fire burst into life, fires were lit in four other countries. The sacred five of Sovereignty connected us all as I sang into the flames and the energy lines of the earth, the Dragon Lines. The intending was for the highest good of all beings through the work that carries me and on the plans for future retreats in all of these five places — Cornwall, Ireland, Canada, Jamaica, and in my homeland of Scotland.

Five years later, in 2019, I stepped for the third time across the threshold of Jackie's on the Reef to work around the fire pit that I had energetically connected with in 2014.

OUR PURPOSE

The reason that Jamaica had called out to me was to help create space in the worlds. It was Jackie who initially contacted me; she had heard about my work with the Dragon Lines and her curiosity was piqued. She wrote to me inviting me to come to the reef and bring a group together to help with personal and planetary healing.

So again, it is threads that lead us to connect to the tapestry and understanding that a much bigger story is unfolding.

My grandmother, who was born in Kemback in the Kingdom of Fife, was illegitimate. That carried a great stigma in Presbyterian Scotland in 1914. She never knew her father and he and his family disowned her. Her father was the son of a Scottish Laird who on his deathbed left her in the early 1970's the equivalent, in today's market, of a million pounds. She refused the money. She labelled it blood money. I later found out years after her death that part of the "blood" she was referring to was that the Laird inherited his fortune from money made on the back of the slave trade.

I also discovered that not only were slaves stolen from their families in Africa, many people from throughout the British Isles and Ireland ended up in the Caribbean in positions of servitude. They were also transported in chains in the bowels of boats lying amongst the vomit and the faeces of their travelling companions. They were whipped and tortured with the only redeeming quality being that their journey of captivity was not infinite, there was a number placed on their years of captivity. As long as they behaved themselves they would one day be set free.

Was it my grandmother or the Laird, my great grandfather, or was it a Universal force that aligned the stars to get me to the Caribbean? I believe that it was all of those and more. I had not envisaged taking a "Celtic" medicine way to Jamaica, Spirit had, the land there and ancestors from other lands as well as my own were screaming for redemption!

Millions of slaves ended up being torn from their lives and loved ones and faced horrendous conditions throughout the Caribbean and the so-called New World.

I was called by the land in Jamaica to help create space and alleviate suffering not only within those who had faced the hardship of slavery, also those who had imposed this hardship upon them. People like my great grandfather's forefathers.

STUCK ENERGY

Here is where it is important for us to examine death. I was brought up with the Christian concept of heaven and hell. Good people go to heaven and bad people go to hell. I began to struggle with the simplicity of this argument when I was told that anyone who took Jesus into their heart as their saviour would go to heaven and anyone who didn't was consigned to hell. Basically, a mass murderer and rapist was granted a pass into the pearly gates as long as they confessed their sins and accepted Christ as their lord, yet someone who had never heard of Christianity from some far remote tribe on the planet was rejected. I questioned what happened to all of the people in pre-Christian times, where did they go?

If you are a Christian, please stay with me as all faiths are called to be part of the evolution. There is space and a place for us all if we are willing to open our hearts to hear each other, to meet each other outside of dogmatic lines.

As I got older I became more attuned to energy work and the Universe opened a doorway for me to help the planet meet and process death. What I have discovered is that there is so much unprocessed death on the planet, so much stuck energy that is screaming for release.

UNPROCESSED DEATH

A saying that is attributed to Benjamin Franklin is commonly thrown out when looking at the guarantees in life — "In this world, nothing can be said to be certain, except death and taxes."

Yet, I believe Franklin misspoke — one of the biggest problems that exists on the planet is unprocessed death, the mere stopping of a heartbeat in itself does not signify death. It is rather the gateway to death.

I have written about this in great detail in *Magical Crows, Ravens and the Celebration of Death*, so if you have already feasted on that story please bear with me as I briefly revisit it again here.

Everything is energy; if you imagine watering the garden via a hose pipe that has water running through it, the water moves from the source, your outside tap/spigot, through the hose and out through the sprinkler. All works wonderfully well until you get a kink in the hose. The more kinks you get the less water flows until the water ceases completely as the hose folds over itself creating many blockages along the way. With a build-up of water, the pressure increases until it bursts out, leaking and splattering in whatever way it can —creating chaos.

When these blockages in the hose occur, what we have is a series of mini dams that I liken to the blockages in our own bodies when death is not fully processed. During our lives, we experience many "living deaths" and the final death of our physical body when our heart stops beating. The question is how do we meet those deaths? Does our fear, pain, anger, and refusal to accept and embrace death block the process? When death is not fully celebrated it remains stuck in process just like the water in the hose, the kinks preventing the flow. Just as in the hose when there is no release for the water, the unprocessed death is unrealised so stagnation occurs with the backup point being our own bodies. The chaos splatters back inside of us and into our daily lives, soaking the community, our families, and the land with all of the unprocessed emotions that are tangled up in a death that has not been fully celebrated!

LIVING DEATHS

I recently was working with a group in Bohannon, Virginia. The night before the group was to meet I was talking to the host who was seeking a deeper understanding of living deaths. I had offered her a mirror exercise that I had learnt from Louise Hay many years ago and which I have shared with thousands of people during my walk on this planet. Again, I have written about the power of this exercise before and even so it is one that can take several visits to fully understand and integrate into our own bodies.

The premise of the exercise is to meet ourselves where we are at. Ultimately, we stand naked in front of a mirror, though to begin with, we approach the mirror fully clothed. We begin with looking into our eyes and speaking aloud from our hearts to ourselves, "I am willing to learn to like you." When and only when this resonates fully in our heart as a truth do we move on.

Next, we meet ourselves with, "I like you, I truly like you." Once this is our heart truth we move to, "I am willing to learn to love you." Until finally we own and celebrate ourselves with, "I love you, I truly love you." Here lies the challenge, so many people want to run before they walk. They will often kid themselves that they are there with the "I love you, I truly love you." They avoid the truth of the feeling that is inside of them seeking to be with what they desire rather than doing the work to get there. In our heads, it can be difficult to own that we do not love ourselves from a place of Sovereignty, a place of the heart. Egotistically we may mask over the truth, gloss it up and fake it, forcing ourselves into a false belief that we love ourselves.

Authenticity is the key and our feelings is what ignites the magic. So if we mask the truth of our feelings we are igniting more unworthiness into our mental and physical bodies which of course affects the spiritual aspect of ourselves.

What helped the host to understand unprocessed death more fully was my response to her admission that looking at herself in the mirror and saying, "I love you, I truly love you," was incredibly difficult. Her focus always went to her wrinkles and how she has aged over the years. Trying to equate the outer picture of herself with her inner self was proving to be nigh impossible.

She, like many people, was failing to come into alignment with the beauty of the ageing process. It is not surprising as society pushes the image of beauty, especially amongst women, into masking over our own skin. The use of make-up has been a constant through the ages, yet disguising and manipulating our features has gone beyond foundation, rouge, mascara, and lipstick to a new norm of lip augmentation and botulinum toxin injection treatments. Add into this mix the number of minor and major surgeries that people undergo to rebuild their faces creating fuller lips, stretching their skin, and ironing out their wrinkles. With leading Hollywood actresses and high profile celebrities redesigning their faces and all of the touch-ups on photographs that distort the reality of a person's complexion and body type in the advertising world, is it any wonder that self-image has drastically reshaped the value of so many people's self-worth?

What I said to her was, "While we yearn to look as young and fresh-faced as we once did, we are in mourning for what was rather than in acceptance of what is. The pain, regret, disappointment or whatever emotional block that is hanging over us prevents us from meeting ourselves in acceptance of what we look like today." I saw a penny drop as she contemplated this information and came to the realisation of how she was stuck in this unprocessed death.

The lines of ageing are a beautiful part of our story, my face is full of laughter lines. My body and face are not at all what one would classify as beautiful or even in the manly world "handsome." I was ridiculed as a kid for being skinny with a big nose, long neck, crooked teeth, and what society likes to call — a weak chin. Yet, in this face of mine I can see pieces of my ancestors; it is a thing of rare beauty, it is uniquely mine, just like each snowdrop has its own signature, so do all of our bodies. When we are willing to grow into them and celebrate them as part of the natural world we live in, honouring each season for the gifts and challenges that come with them in acceptance and love, we change the landscape of our world.

I went on to say how you find people stuck in so many stories. The person who returns to a holiday destination desperately trying to recreate a past holiday that was the best one of their lives. Instead of letting the past go and celebrating a new adventure, they crave what they perceive they have lost. Unprocessed death lingers whenever relationships end and a celebration fails to occur. There are many examples, here are a few in a much longer list — losing a loved one in either the death of their body or in the ending of friendships, marriages/partnerships or love affairs, moving homes, changing schools, being made redundant, changing jobs, failing to get a job, being cut from or failing to make the team, getting rejected for a part in a play. There are myriad shifts in circumstances that each of us faces in our lifetimes that lead to deep sorrow, anger, pain, jealousy, frustration, resentment, and other tangled emotions that if left unchecked and unprocessed, manifest as blockages in our bodies.

CHANGING THE PATTERN

I was gifted a medicine way several years ago to change the pattern, by transmuting the dark threads that come under the umbrella of sorrow into joy and then into peace. I will speak more of this anon; however, right now I would like to stay with the idea of unprocessed death and the challenges that are faced because of them.

WHEN OUR HEART STOPS BEATING

Then, of course, there is the ultimate death of our bodies. The temple that some say houses our soul, however, many mystics through the ages have argued that the heart is in the body and the body is in the soul and the soul journeys to the ends of the world.

There are two pieces I would like to focus on here.
Firstly, what if the mystics are right? I remember
discussing this with one of my teachers, Tom Cowan,
many moons ago. The idea of oneness came up, the
idea that only a small percentage of who I am is
happening within my own body temple, the rest, the
larger percentage is being all of the other aspects of
myself. I am a crest of the wave, I am a hawk in flight,
I am the sun's rays kissing myself as the morning dew.
I will also return to this idea and explore it in more
depth later.

Secondly, what happens to the soul aspect of myself
when my physical body temple shuts down? Is there
life after death? From my perspective there is,
however, just like the living deaths that are
unprocessed, there is also a copious amount of
unprocessed death around the deaths of our physical
bodies. This has caused major blockages in the land,
air, and waters of our planet.

How does this work? A body that shuts down releases a soul that when free from earthly attachments passes over, it goes home. My understanding of this is it goes to the source. It returns to the light. If it is an easier concept to relate to then call it Heaven, Svarga Loka, Trayastrimsa, Valhalla, or whatever works within your cosmology for the afterlife. It is a place where all beings are welcome yet so many fail to reach because death has not been fully realised.

Possession, trauma, and attachment all play a role in tethering a soul to an unprocessed death.

Does this sound far-fetched to you? If so, I invite you to await judgement until you consider what I am about to share here.

TRAUMA

If we look through the history of the modern world, it is based on wars and occupation. One civilization imposing their ideas on another. Alongside the desire to claim more land came the spoils of war, the rape and pillage of both humans and the land. Slavery has been a mainstay of human conquest and the animal, vegetable, and mineral kingdoms have suffered great loss, pain, and destruction alongside millions of humans who have been slaughtered in the name of a "righteous" war!

When death comes upon us in a fashion whereby it is sudden, unexpected and/or traumatic, the soul has to had less time to digest the fact and to come to terms with no longer having a body. Albeit a car accident, a plane crash, a mass shooting in a school, an earthquake, a bombing, deforestation, slaughtering livestock, even a suicide, which may have been planned and yet the depth of despair can so easily block the person from celebrating death because of unresolved issues connecting them to the trauma of the event. The atrocities associated with modern warfare are well documented with millions of innocents caught in the crossfire and mass genocide occurring in different parts of the globe during my lifetime and that of my parents and grandparents.

As we look further back into time we find in each age, Stone, Bronze, and Iron a constant desecration of beings upon the planet as humans have looked to defend what they have won. Emperors, Kings, Queens, Pharaohs, Sultans, and the like have mustered the masses into fighting one another for the good of the tribe, region, or country that they have claimed as their own. A god given right was taken up as their war cry and by sharing the spoils with their most trusted supporters a hierarchy was formed which still affects our world today. The names may have changed to Presidents, Prime Ministers, Chairmen and the like, yet the premise remains the same: an elite group shape the world and expect the collective to bow and serve the war machine. The biggest players lurk in the shadows acting as puppeteers, often pulling the strings of the figureheads that are supposedly in charge.

War makes money, it is good for business and one way to keep the masses subdued is to stir the pot of nationalism which ultimately leads to separation. There is a fine line between how we honour the remembrance of our past stories and how we get tethered to them. Unfortunately, we have established patterns whereby war is glorified.

ATTACHMENTS

One of the ways that we struggle to let go of our body temples when we die are the strong attachments we have made in our lives. We connect energetic cords to beings, places, and things. Sometimes our love is so strong for another being that when they are ready to go we cling desperately to them begging them not to leave us. As I write this, there are beings being kept alive through drugs or machines though the quality of life is long gone. Why? The loved ones alive are simply not ready to let go. This happens with people and their animals as well as between people themselves.

When the being is finally released from their body temple they can get trapped in the feelings of those they are leaving behind as well as their own unresolved feelings. If this sounds strange look at how it happens amongst the living. There are people on the planet who stay in a relationship when the love has long gone because of feelings of guilt, duty, and a sense of honour. Why would it be any different after death?

On a larger scale, the way we remember stories can create stuck energy. I have cited Culloden in previous writings as an example of this. For those who are unfamiliar with Culloden, it is a moor in Scotland where a battle took place between the English crown and the Scottish Jacobite army. It was a massacre whereby over 1,200 of the Jacobite army were slaughtered within an hour, many more were badly wounded compared to the handful of the Loyalist forces who died or were injured.

This took place on April 16, 1746, which led to the Highland clearances. The trauma of this battle still affects Scotland to this day.

Troublemakers were hung or thrown into chains and transported on boats to the New World in positions of servitude. The Scottish clan tartans were taken away, their language, instruments, and songs banished. Sheep became more profitable than people and for Ancient Alba, modern-day Scotland, this time became a trail of tears.

If you visit the battleground today, the energy of the massacre is still tangible for those sensitive to feel it. The visitors' centre at the battleground plays a video reconstruction of this massacre several times each day. Hereby we preserve history and yet we replay the horror of what occurred here over and over again.

My thoughts on this is that we create energy nodes on the planet that either liberate and free beings or become magnets for the blocked energy to flock to.

I see this bleak and eerie strip of moorland as a magnet for lost souls to congregate. When I lived in Pennsylvania I was struck by a similar feeling when walking the battlefield at Gettysburg where 10,000 Union and Confederate soldiers perished in a bloody battle that took place over three days in July 1863.

All across the planet, there are pockets of trapped energy, some more concentrated than others.

It is not about forgetting the stories of our past. It is about celebrating death so new life can be birthed. In the case of Culloden, it is about transforming the Scottish trail of tears from tears of sorrow to tears of joy so that peace can flow.

As I have stated, my intending is to share how we can do this; however, before I do, it is important to examine why it is important to do so!

Within all of this, I do not want to diminish the importance of remembering our history whereby we provide a memorial, a memory of honouring our ancestors. However, I believe that it is <u>how</u> we remember them that is the key to allowing us all to heal. Providing cultural experiences that celebrate life as in the planting of indigenous trees, the sharing of music, song, poetry, stories, dance, and art resonate in my heart. Revisiting the atrocities, recreating them, and replaying them perpetuates the sorrow.

Again, I invite you to look at the world and ask yourself whether you feel there is more sorrow, anger, and darkness of emotions swirling around in the world or is there more authentic joy, love, and generosity of spirit? What kind of news stories feed our society from the journalists and media?

DIVISION

Not only are countries pitted against countries, we have patterns of division woven into our stories within many of these countries. I look at my own birthplace, England, whereby there is a north/south divide.

I look at my ancestral bloodlines that are split between Scotland and England and see the divide between two nations that are under the umbrella of the U.K. During an Olympic gold medal ceremony, all members of the U.K. share the national anthem of "God Save the Queen." An anthem that in a latter verse includes the line — "And in a torrent rush, rebellious Scots to crush, God save the Queen!"

In our desperation to belong to this group or that we so often alienate others. Quick judgements are made the moment words sprout from our lips depending on the accent that comes forth.

As a football/soccer fan, I look at the events that unfolded recently with players from the England team being racially abused in a game in Montenegro. There was an outcry in the British press against Eastern European countries for their bigotry. A former English footballer, John Barnes, tempered this outburst with a timely reminder stating, "It's hypocritical for us in this country to look at Montenegro and say how terrible it is when it happens every week in this country."

Football/soccer is our nation's top sport and is also listed as the world's number one sport with over four billion followers, yet apparently, there are no high profile, so-called "stars," who are gay. Why not? Because of the vilification of the tribal nature of the fans. The abuse a player would receive has kept the sexuality of many firmly under lock and key.

Plainly put, we have co-created a planet of masks, war, and division rather than a planet of authenticity, peace, and inclusion.

POSSESSION

I was talking to my dad about his teenage years and he shared that he used to have one shirt and one pair of underpants to last him through the week, my how times have changed. It is amazing how many things we collect in this day and age. I wonder how many of you have garages that are choc-a-bloc with boxes of stuff, attics that are brimming to burst, basements stacked high, sheds bulging at the seams, and cupboards in every room of the house packed full.

I warrant that for many of us space is a premium! I would go as far as to say that many people have boxes in their possession whereby they are unaware of what is inside.

The industrial revolution provided an accessibility to manufacture and produce more possessions at reduced rates which have added not only to the number of goods on the planet, it has meant that pollution has skyrocketed. We manufacture goods that are made to break. Apparently, it is not good business to make and supply something that someone will only ever buy once; if we build equipment to fall apart then we build a successful business that is worth investing in.

For example, I am perplexed at the quality of my new iMac; it is not only more flimsy than my old one, the keyboard feels cheap in comparison, the ports on the side of the computer are different meaning that none of my USB drives or cables will fit it. Apparently, I now have to buy adaptors! The old adage "if it ain't broken don't fix it" has long been thrown out with the bathwater.

The quick-fix age has led to laziness and sloppiness. "I can just buy/get another one" is the norm. Airports sell bottled water like hot cakes, airline companies serve drinks in throwaway containers, and trying to locate a water fountain inside the airport is challenging. How many of us carry a tea/coffee cup with us wherever we go and a receptacle for our drinking water? I do not see many people refusing or reusing plastic in airports!

And the amount of plastic that is in the average home in the Western world is staggering.

It is not only the craving for more goods that is the problem created with possession, but it is also our desire for ownership of land and our relationship with that land. When we rip the Earth up at the expense of other life forms and the wellbeing of the Earth itself, there will naturally be a consequence. The manipulation and invasion of the planet through pollutants and an attitude of me, me, me, mine, mine, mine has to be answered for somewhere along the line.

People also look to possess other people. I have mentioned an obvious example here of the modern day slave trade; however, the subtleties of possession spill into local communities. I recently received an email from a student who has been told by her boss that if she upholds a long-term commitment that she has to travel to Scotland for her education that there will be no job for her to come back to. Her travel plans are not new to the company; however, the company has scheduled something new that they expect her to make a priority. I wonder how many people are treated in such an indispensable way and how many cow down to their employers who lord it over them?

Then there is the possession of children to consider. How many youngsters are told what profession they are to undertake in their lives, how many feel the weight of family expectation upon them?

And what about couples who treat their partners as their possessions, the "trophy" wives or the controlling partners who dictate where their mate goes and what they wear. Even the devoted lovers who simply cannot let go when their partner takes their last breath. So many people tethered by other beings and by their own inability to let go of the trappings of life.

SPACE

With so many beings over the eons of the story of the planet not fully passing over, we have a multitude of what we call lost or displaced souls.

This extends beyond humankind to all of the animals who face terrifying deaths, trees that are hacked down. Perhaps you do not believe all sentient beings have a soul, what if they do though? What if our past is blocking our future because of a lack of space in the present?

And what about all of the living deaths that are unprocessed? Where does that stuck energy reside? As I arrived at Jackie's on the Reef I was shown a clear picture of how all of this works and it began with the importance of creating space.

CHAPTER 3: ANCESTRAL SONG

CREATING SPACE

Having been to Jackie's twice before I was excited to cross the threshold of the sanctuary that would be my room for my stay on the reef. It is a unique space, a resplendent dome-shaped room which my partner Joyce and I had shared on both previous visits.

The dome is a special space, it is separated from the rest of the retreat centre and offers commanding views of the reef and the Caribbean Sea. There is a large mesh screen that takes up one full side of the space, it affords you an opportunity to feel like you are outside while being under the protection of a thatched roof with coral walls. The dome was created from a design by Buckminster Fuller based on nature and sacred geometry. When you lay in bed you can look through a skylight up towards the stars and best of all is the sound of the ocean lapping onto the shore that leads you into the dreamtime.

It is a slice of luxury and a much-appreciated sanctuary for me when leading retreats for as much as I love being around the participants, it is important to be able to sequester myself away and get downtime. Having space for myself allows me to give more to those who attend.

On this occasion, Joyce had not travelled with me and when I met Jackie she suggested that as I was on my own the dome could be used by a couple and I could take the cottage. The cottage is a great space yet does not afford the space and privacy of the dome. An old pattern of mine would be to step aside and let someone else have the sumptuousness of the dome; however, a voice spoke loudly inside of me of the importance of space and how claiming it at that moment would benefit all beings.

VOICES FROM SPIRIT

Listening to the small still voice of Spirit guides my work. How do we do this? Firstly, this is not an exclusive skill, I believe we are all capable of this, it is not only a selected few who have this ability. It is something that requires practice if we wish to hone our ability. My years of leading pilgrimages out on the land, taking days of silence in the wild outdoor spaces, multiple times each year, and my work as a shamanic leader and practitioner has helped me hone this skill.

Had I have taken the room through ego I am sure that what unfolded next would have been a different story. I didn't take the room to have something bigger and better than, I took the room because Spirit was guiding me to create space on many levels. This was a step into doing exactly that on a physical level which would lead to the mental and spiritual aspects that were about to be shown to me.

WHAT IS SHAMANISM?

Like all labels, defining what I do in the world by using one can get lost in translation. Shamanism is a term that may sound strange to some readers while being very familiar to others. For me, shamanism is simply a term I use for those who are connected to working with the wellbeing of the Earth to benefit all sentient beings.

Someone who lives a shamanic lifestyle and teaches others has a huge responsibility as a guardian of the planet. They have the ability to walk between the worlds, to connect with the ancestors and with unseen beings, they are medicine people. And there are many amongst this tribe of beings who can see the tapestry of life clearly, others who, like myself, dedicate their lives in service for the highest good of all beings.

What it is not is a religious cult that is backwards thinking and full of devil worship. For me, it is a spiritual practice that at its core is not harnessed by any dogma that can be found in some religious circles.

Because its heart is in the welfare of all beings, it is all-encompassing. I have witnessed in myself and other students of shamanism an evolution of many aspects of ourselves as it requires us to walk into our own shadow sides to take our light there. It is a constant process requiring the willingness to go deeper so we can ultimately vibrate at a higher frequency when holding space for ourselves and others. It certainly isn't an easy pathway, in some ways, it is like the sea; in the hands of someone who is not coming from the heart it can be destructive, it can splatter and create more chaos in the worlds. In the hands and heart of someone who is a hollow bone, allowing Spirit to flow into them, it cleanses, smoothing away the rough edges so we can reflect more of our light in the worlds.

In all fields of life, human beings can twist something that in its purest form — is a service provided for the highest good of all beings, into something that is self-serving and ultimately calamitous. As in all professions, shamanic teachers and practitioners choose to operate in light or darkness or somewhere in-between. Like leaders in all organisations, there are those who look to serve through the goodness in their hearts and others who commit atrocities. Yet in all cases, as I regularly share with students, do not put any teachers/leaders regardless of their profession on a pedestal. Why not? Because we are all human and we will fall off. We are all works in progress!

One thing is for sure the infighting and ego-driven aspects of the "healing community" will not serve the evolution of our species and the planet. This applies to the wider community, for those who tear down a shamanic teacher or practitioner because of fear and a lack of understanding will ultimately cause more tangles in the web of life. Jabbing and stabbing at something that is outside of our sphere of understanding and ripping it apart only leads to chaos. In this fragile time on the planet, a closed heart edges us further towards extinction!

HOLLOW BONE

What is a hollow bone? It is a clear pathway for Spirit to bring the work through us. It is in dropping the ego and connecting into the elements that make up our bodies that we offer Spirit access to flow. When I am rooted deeply into the Earth and connected to the breath of Spirit through the heavens, I allow the energies of the Earth to come through my feet and flow through the waters of my physical body into my heart flame, my fire. As I do this I bring the air and the light of the Milky Way through my head so that it also blesses the waters of my body and connects to my heart. With my heart flame ignited, my fire and waters create a rainbow of light. This multi-coloured spectrum connects Spirit through me to all of creation.

VISION FROM SPIRIT

My first full day in Jamaica began with a massage. I knew that I would be plucking the three strands of poetry, an indigenous way of creating space in our bodies as we keen, wail, release all of the emotional strands that are placed under the banner of sorrow into joy and then peace. I will outline this process in more detail later. For now, I would like to stay with this vision that I received after creating space from both settling into the dome room and from the massage. A full body massage opens up so much space as knots from life's tensions and stress are kneaded away.

I returned to the sanctuary of the dome as sitting in the full Jamaica sun is not for a lily white body type like myself. Where the first day on our arrival had heralded torrential rains, the second day was all about strong winds. Sitting in the dome was a totally cleansing experience as the wind whistled through the room blowing some of my clothes off of the hangers.

The weather conditions percolated inside of me. I mulled over the strength of the waters on our day of arrival, not only from the rainfall also from the waves crashing in from the sea. On this day, I sat with the element of air as we were buffeted by high winds. As I watched the white horses on the sea and the foam kissing the land, I revisited my conversation with Pat in regards to the Earth, the elements, and the lymphatic gland.

It was then that I got clear images of all of the sludge that has been poured into the air, the waters, and the land through the ages. All of the toxins from pollutants including the toxicity of the human mind.

All of this anger, frustration, rage, fear, hatred, abuse, pain, and all of the other emotions that are tangled into the bundles of sorrow that scream so loudly on the planet have to go somewhere. They have seeped into the pores of the planet — the earth, the air, the water, and the fires of our home are fit to burst, we are running out of space!

Both in the visible and invisible realms our world is congested. The strand of sorrow drips and bleeds within and without. The silent screams are deafening!

Another part of the equation that many people might overlook or not even be aware of is the unprocessed death which includes countless lost and displaced souls.

In our living world if we open our eyes it is obvious to see that so many animal populations are running out of space because of the ever-increasing population boom amongst us humans. Space is a premium both in the seen aspects of life and in the unseen.

Is it too far a stretch for the imagination to comprehend that the inner aspects of the Earth have become clogged with pollutants from the physical and the mental and also from the spiritual? With the inner fighting that has brought a division in spirituality by focusing on whose religion is right and whose is wrong, we have created toxins on an unparalleled scale. Our mental state is clearly tipped towards anxiety, fear, anger, etc. and our physical bodies ingest so much junk food and preservatives. Are you able to correlate how we as a species affect the whole? Are you able to relate to how our clogged bodies are impacting our planet in devastating ways?

The planet is unable to breathe because its pores are blocked. The way the Earth will respond is to create ways to cleanse and breathe. This means eruptions of cataclysmic proportions. Mass earthquakes, floods, tsunamis, forest fires, tornadoes, hurricanes, volcanic eruptions, the Earth will look to reinvent itself, the Earth will go through its own evolution with us or without us. If we continue down the pathway that we have been on, then it will be without us. I tasted the emotions under the umbrella of sorrow that was tangible on the wind, I saw them in the sea, I felt them in the Earth. So many beings will be swallowed up as the Earth looks to protect and purify itself.

It is already happening, the ice caps are melting at an alarming rate and there are many natural disasters springing up around the globe. This may have caught our attention, however, what I was shown was that this is on a small scale compared to the mass devastation upon the horizon.

As desperate as this series of images was it was followed by a clearing, a space for homo-sapiens to reinvent themselves. A space where we get to choose a different pathway. A space to re-dream, remember, reweave, rebirth, and recreate a new world. I had an inner knowing that we *can*, it may seem a small shift from hope to knowing yet it felt expansive in all of my bodies. I was dancing within and without with this new found knowledge.

I wasn't shown what the end result is, only that it is through our hearts that we can activate a medicine way of change. The Earth is ready for the dreamers, the visionaries and the sacred outcasts to bring their gift of song, their dance, their music, their poetry, their laughter, their unadulterated love, and joy to be the evolution of not only this world: it will liberate other worlds connected to this world.

Sound implausible? Well, stay with me for what happened next took my knowing to a much deeper level and allowed the teachings of this retreat to impact the whole community that had gathered in a (r)evolutionary way!

THE HIGH SEA

My third day in Jamaica was Valentine's Day and my good friends, Mike and Jenn Fenster, who had flown in the night before, had rented out a forty-two foot Catalina Yacht and had invited Joyce and myself to accompany them on a voyage across the high seas. As you are aware Joyce wasn't with me, what you may not know is I don't get on boats for pleasure cruises. I do not have my sea legs. I learned early in life that my love of the sea is from a vantage point of the land. Take me on a boat and the slightest swell ends up with me feeding the fish.

However, when there is a spiritual purpose I will gladly climb aboard. I have braved the crossing to Skellig Michael five times in my life. It is a hairy crossing to a magical island that for a brief period of the summer is inhabited by thousands of puffins. Ascending barefoot on the pilgrim path of 618 stone steps is profound. This stairway to the gods was carved into the rock by monks who made this remote island their home from the 6th to the 12th century. Beehive huts are perched high on the summit of this tiny island off of the mainland of Ireland. I have not made a single crossing without leaning over the side and retching, normally within ten minutes of setting sail.

When Mike and Jenn emailed to invite Joyce and me to join them we were delighted to say yes, as at that time we all thought Joyce would be with us. The draw was not to go sailing though it was important to me that it was a sailboat, even more important was knowing that the engine aboard was powered by solar energy. The draw was not a romantic voyage on Valentine's Day where the plan was to sail around

Jamaica and have dinner at a restaurant on the beach as the sun went down. The draw was to sail into port in a way that the ancestors who had been transported to the Caribbean during the slave trade had never experienced. I was called to let them see joy through my eyes, to reach the shore with a feeling of freedom and celebration rather than fear and incarceration. This was worth going to sea for and I am forever grateful to Mike and Jenn for offering this experience to me.

With Joyce staying home in Scotland, the Fensters kindly extended the invitation to my friend Pat to join us. A car duly arrived early in the morning to take us to join Mike and Jenn, who had slept on the boat the night before, in Montego Bay.

The owner of the yacht, Carolyn, who was our driver, shared how she had recently sailed the boat from Boston to Key West and then on from Florida to Montego Bay.

After a day of heavy rain and a day of strong winds, we were greeted to the weather that I had remembered from my previous two visits to Jamaica which had both also been in February — glorious sunshine. On route, I chatted with Carolyn about my non-sea legs and how the waves on the reef the previous two days had not looked good for a smooth sail. She looked to ease my concerns of a rough sail by pointing out that weather conditions off of Negril were completely different to those off Montego Bay.

She was right, the water looked like a mill pond and bright smiling faces greeted us as we walked up the wooden dock towards our ride where Mike, Jenn, the captain, and first mate of the stellar looking yacht named the Wind Horse were eagerly awaiting our arrival.

MAGNIFYING THE MAGIC

I knew this day was going to be an important one. Having received the visions from the day before I was buoyed with anticipation. The signs from the Universe leading me to this point in my life were strong. I had been connecting the many dots including how on this third visit to Jamaica I had opened up the retreat to involve more people.

The previous two gatherings had been powerful and intense. We had worked with creating space — singing home displaced and lost souls and charging up the energy grid of the Earth known as the Dragon Lines. The major difference this time was I had invited people from all around the globe to send their prayers in for personal and planetary healing.

All prayers would be read out loud into the 13-hour birthing fire planned in five-days' time on the full moon. My intending was to speak the prayers into the fire twice through the night and then at the zenith of the moon at 10.53am on February 19th, all of the prayers would be wrapped up into a bundle and placed into the flames.

The sheer act of inviting people to send in their prayers and then go a step further by lighting a candle or hearth fire to join us in the ethers during this ceremony had magnified everything.

I carried prayers from people in Australia, South America, Central America, North America, throughout mainland Europe, India, Jamaica, the U.K., and Ireland. People of all faiths from devout Christians to Pagans, Muslims to Buddhists, from millennials to elders all brought together with a flame of hope for our world. I also carried prayers from other leading shamanic teachers from across the world and I felt the swell of numbers exceeding the count of prayers because of the communities that are connected to these beings.

I could feel the energy tangibly vibrating in and around me. Just as I had a sense of knowing that we can re-dream the worlds, I knew that this gathering was going to play a significant role in changing the way I, and those who were working with me, will walk on the planet.

PAYING ATTENTION TO THE LITTLE THINGS

Magic happens in the little things that can often go unnoticed yet when added together into the story illuminate the tapestry in compelling ways. As I stood in front of the Wind Horse the captain bade me to swing my backpack over to him before I boarded the stern. As I slipped the backpack off it suddenly slid down my arms and the straps got tangled in a bracelet on my wrist. I was trapped as my hands came together behind my back and things started to fall out of the open side pockets of the bag. It took Carolyn interceding, reaching down and freeing my wrists and hands from the bondage that I found myself in.

The Jamaican captain, Mark, then took the bag off me and once it was stored he reached out a hand to help me aboard. As we left the harbour, I sat with the power of the symbolism that had struck me as soon as this event had taken place. The ancestors were well and truly with me. My intending was to sail back to shore so they could see through my eyes and we could dance in the beauty of freedom. To do so I had become the vessel for them all to experience freedom through me and the first thing that had to happen was to remove the shackles of their enslavement!

With the mainsail hoisted Mike Fenster called out to the captain, "Sail us off the edge of the map!" The four of us passengers walked out towards the bow and the thrill of gliding across a calm clear sea brought expansion into my bodies to match the billowing sails.

As we headed out to sea a magnificent frigate bird flew across our path. Its nickname was not lost on me for in the Caribbean they are known as Man-of-War birds.

The turquoise and vibrant blue waters licked gently onto the Wind Horse and I was grateful to feel grounded aboard a boat and not be feeding the fish, especially on an empty stomach having missed breakfast. I had eaten a banana and an energy bar to tide me over; it is never pleasant to retch especially on an empty stomach.

Our captain and first mate were knowledgeable and offered the best of Jamaican hospitality. When Mark dropped anchor Bobby talked through the techniques of snorkelling. I nearly drowned when I was a young boy and putting my head underwater is quite the challenge, swimming out of my depth in the sea even with a life jacket on is not a comfortable thought. However, the opportunity to snorkel for the first time in my life outweighed any of my old fears of drowning.

It was also important to take to the waters for the ancestors. To swim freely amongst the colours of a world that I had not witnessed before and they most certainly would have not seen. And what a world! If you have never experienced the glory of swimming with schools of brightly coloured fish, I can thoroughly recommend it. The brightest blues, oranges, yellows, and a variety of stripes bedazzled my senses. As I floated above them the fish came within grazing reach of me. Bobby would call out from time to time to come towards where the water was crystal clear. Because of the torrential rains that had hit the coast, there was a cloudy film that one needed to swim beneath to find the clarity that is often apparent in these seas.

Pat and I talked about that when we were back on board the Wind Horse looking at the symbolism of going deeper into a medicine way so that we can see things more clearly.

As I swam back towards the yacht I felt the presence of mer-people swimming beside me.

UNSEEN BEINGS

If you do not believe in the existence of mermaids and mermen, then who am I to dispute and mock your belief. On the flip side of the coin why would it be okay to mock mine? I was born in the "Celtic" Isles where we have a long tradition of faerie tales. There are families in Scotland who will swear that their ancestry is from the mer-people. It wasn't many years ago that more people in the British Isles and Ireland freely admitted to a belief in the wee folk, the gentry, the sidhe, the faerie beings that inhabit our world. In pockets people still do. There is certainly a fascination with them and a host of stories that extends across the whole globe. In Jamaica at Roaring River, there is a well-preserved legend of Miriam the mermaid who lives in the waters that flow through the earth there and out to the sea.

So before you slam the book closed and dismiss something that you have never seen or felt as mere fancy, I invite you to journey on into the unknown with me. I was fortunate in having a happy childhood and unlike many adults, I have carried the joy of playfulness into my adulthood. My early years were not censored so when I would go for a walk in the woods where the Fae danced no-one told me I was delusional and wrong. My receptors stayed open to sensing, feeling, and also seeing glimpses of the unseen beings that live within the veil.

SKY JUICE

Once we were all aboard we sailed on until Pat started to get sea-sick. The swells on the water were choppier and Mark decided to head back to shore so we could anchor there for lunch. I had a chance to speak to Mark prior to my snorkelling adventure and on the way back to port I got to talk with Bobby. Both of them have found their vocation in life, they love the sea and have forged a life whereby they feel as free as the wind propelling the Wind Horse's sails across the waves. I talked fondly of being fortunate enough in my life to see Bob Marley and the Wailers live in 1980 at the Crystal Palace Bowl in London. It was there that I learned what "sky juice" is. There was a trader shouting "sky juice, watermelon, sky juice" I was intrigued and went over to find out that sky juice was bottled water! Bobby laughed and asked if I liked Burning Spear. With delight, I shared that my favourite track of theirs is from the album Hail H.I.M — "Columbus." Bobby then burst into song, "Christopher Columbus is a damn blasted liar!" The laughter and joy overflowed as we anchored by the shore for lunch.

Mark prepared a feast, although Pat wasn't up for eating as her stomach was still churning. Mike and Jenn devoured fish while I gobbled up a veggie platter in honour of the ancestors. Before we set sail again a song that was playing in the cabin below caught my attention. I had ventured below deck to use the toilet. Mark had music blaring out and as Spirit would have it, Bob Marley was singing "Redemption Song." It was with great delight that Mark and I started dancing and singing to this classic anthem that I was fortunate enough to hear live when Bob and the Wailers had ended their set with it back in 1980 at the Bowl. I continued singing and dancing from below decks up onto the bow. I felt high on life as I sang with gusto inviting all beings to help me sing songs of freedom. What a way to honour the ancestors, what a buzz it was for me to know they were experiencing such joy and freedom through my eyes, my heart, my bones.

CHAPTER 4: THE EDGE OF THE MAP

TWO SIDES TO EVERY STORY

It hadn't occurred to me until things shifted that by setting the intending for the ancestors to see arriving into Jamaica through my eyes that they would choose to share arriving into port through their eyes. It wasn't long after setting sail that a story of two halves unfolded. The weather dramatically changed. The mill pond that had been replaced by light swells was now favouring white horses that licked and kicked their foam spraying over the bow. I had been sitting with Mike on the starboard side and chose to move into the sunken seats at the stern as it was too choppy for me.

My thoughts had turned to dry land as my stomach was beginning to churn. I remember saying, "This is rough enough thank you!" and Mike replying, "Bring it on!" Mike is a water lover and an adventurous soul like myself. We both have a love of dancing on the edge yet my mind hovered over his words thinking — be careful what you wish for. I noticed that he had taken his hat off and was holding it in his hands. We are both eccentric beings. He is a heart surgeon, gourmet chef, and author who wears a frock coat and tricorn hat wherever he travels. I have seen him in this outfit in a snowstorm in Calgary, from photos of his travels in Africa, in the "four seasons in one-day" weather of the Isle of Skye, Scotland and now here in Jamaica on the Caribbean Sea.

He had offered me a dram of rum earlier in the day and I had declined. I drink very little alcohol in life as I never know when Spirit will require me to be available and fully present to be the work of a medicine way.

I left him to enjoy the stormy waters that gave him such a thrill as I sought the sanctuary of the seating in the stern. We had been heading to a different port for supper, however, that was nixed as Mark now turned the boat around choosing to head back to Montego Bay instead.

Jenn had disappeared into the bowels of the boat to get changed in the bedroom that was underneath the bow and Pat was lying down on the port side in the sunken seated area opposite me in the stern. I was suddenly called to phone Joyce who was back home in Scotland. The weather had turned dramatically cold and as the water became increasingly turbulent the boat suddenly flipped so that the sail was leaning towards the sea. Not knowing anything about sailing my first thought was, is this what people do for fun?

We seemed to pick up speed and as I was on the side of the boat that was elevated I found myself clinging onto a rail above my head and bracing my feet against the seat opposite me. I was concerned that I needed to hold on with both hands and that the phone in my hands could easily end up in the sea so I carefully tucked it into a small day bag that was strung around my neck. Pat was laying down leaning into the support of the backrest of the bench seat, trying to move was not an option for her as she would have fallen into the guard rail that was precariously close to the water. I later learned that this tipping of the yacht is known as *heeling* and is a usual procedure when going into or towards the wind.

Inside my inner radar was telling me that something here was not right. Underneath the boat is a large fin-shaped piece known as a *keel* that has a big weight on the end to allow the boat to heel without tipping over. However, there is a tipping point that the keel can no longer resist. If you reach that point the yacht will capsize. It seemed to me that we were a hairs breath away from reaching our tipping point.

I later found out that my instincts were correct. Mark suddenly called an order to Mike to move off the starboard side into the seating area as he needed to tack, which means change direction. It was then that the sh-t hit the fan. As a non-sailor, I am still struggling to understand all of the terms. What was described to me though was that you never want to end up broadside in a stormy sea and that was exactly where we were at.

As Mark looked to make the manoeuvre Bobby went to adjust a rope on the sail. The boat sprang back upright, there was a huge gust of wind the rigging went loose and a rope snapped. The violence of the wind ripped and tore the jib sail and the loose rope whipped through the air shattering the Perspex screen that shielded those inside the seating area of the stern. The jib didn't tear all of the way, it was caught up at the end. The flailing rope lashed towards us narrowly missing my face and the yacht's radar was tossed overboard. Mark was trying to sail us one way and the jib was taking us another way.

We were looking death squarely in the face. If we had panicked I believe this story would have rested along with my bones at the bottom of the sea. As I wrote this I got quite emotional in understanding the mechanics of what transpired sailing the yacht through this storm. The full impact of how perilously close we were from flipping over hit me. Yet, I had left out a part of the equation, the piece that changed everything in my world, the piece that had given me every confidence that we would safely negotiate our passage — the voice of Spirit!

AMRUN

All indigenous societies have a song that sings us, a Spirit song that has no fixed melody, tune, or words. It is a freedom song that comes through a medicine person and those working a medicine way. The singer gets out of the way, they become a hollow bone and allow the voice of Spirit to flow through them.

In the "Celtic" world this song is known as *Amrun*. I first discovered Amrun or perhaps I should say Amrun rediscovered me as a child. I did not understand then the multi-dimensional purpose of this medicine or even that it was a medicine way. I remember that it was liberating and brought me much joy. I cannot recall when I began my journey with Amrun, it has always been with me for as long as I can remember. It was a private journey for me in those days. I would open up myself to the song that sings me when I was alone in the woods or in a wild place in nature. It was later in my life that I discovered a shamanic pathway and in so doing realised that I also came from a line of indigenous people. We tend to forget in Europe that our ancestors carried medicine bundles outside of modern medicine, that we had wise ones amongst us who were in tune with the elements, who were in tune with the song of the Earth.

A paragraph from an ancient text that the monks scribed from earlier "Celtic" stories gave me a word that named this medicine way in our tradition. In the epic of *The Second Battle of Mag Tuired*, five members of the Tuatha Dé Danann climb a hill and for a year and a day they work with the magical strands of Amrun. Giving this medicine an ancestral name has heightened and deepened this song that emanates through me.

For many years now I have worked with Amrun and I have found that it has multi-dimensional properties. It is a wonderful tool that helps to transmute and transform. I have shared this way with thousands of people across the globe and I work with it in many ways from powering up the Dragon Lines, singing home the souls of the dead, personal healing work in my own bodies, and in other being's bodies and as a way of communicating with nature. Yet, I had never worked with it to weave protection around myself and other beings before. It hadn't occurred to me because I had never been in a position to work with it in this way.

On board the Wind Horse that day it wasn't a conscious decision to sing Amrun, in the heat of battle it came flowing through. All my years of being a vessel for Spirit had prepared me to open my heart and weave with this medicine in this brand new way.

As I reflect back now it took everybody on board to do, to be what they could be in that moment. Jenn stayed below deck by the radio transmitter awaiting a call from Mark to send out a Mayday distress call. Mike grabbed hold of the flapping sail and held onto it for all he was worth. Mark was at the wheel while

Bobby embarked on a precarious journey towards the sails with a view to taking them down.

The boat bobbed furiously and Bobby danced on the deck as the rope which I have learned technically is called a *line*, whipped around his feet. If the line wrapped around his body he would be catapulted into an unforgiving sea.

I set an intending of protection around the boat and around all of us on the boat. Amrun is heart medicine, had I been in my head I would have got in the way of the flow. I opened my mouth and became an instrument for Spirit to work through me. Beside me, Pat who has travelled with me in seven countries and has worked alongside me for over twenty years joined me in the song of Amrun.

She said later that she went way down into the depth of the sea where still waters run deep. She became that stillness and the stillness became her. With strands of protection weaved around the Wind Horse, my full concentration was on protecting Bobby. Pat spoke afterwards how the pelting rain felt more like sleet, it was only when we were out of danger did I realize how cold I was. With Spirit flowing through me I was like a furnace. Mike had got his wish — we had sailed off the edge of the map — or it sure felt like we had. The coastline of Jamaica disappeared, the sea was angry. Frothing foam spat at us from the waves that no longer glistened blue — they darkened to black. Visibility lessened to ten feet as driving rain and mist closed in on us. And then the sails were down and there was a breath, a space of knowing that we had come through the gateway of death.

SPIRIT AT THE WHEEL

However, the Amrun continued to flow for now a new danger was on our horizon. The radar that had been launched overboard was an expensive commodity to leave behind and Mark was determined to retrieve it.

Bobby had grabbed a large pole with a hook on it and was desperately trying to reach out to snag the radar while looking to maintain his balance and stay aboard the Wind Horse. The Amrun was flowing around him as I concentrated on an energetic lifeline that would prevent him from being flung into the raging sea. Mark was on the wheel riding each wave swinging the boat around again and again. Each time we got close, the communication device evaded Bobby's hook. The Wind Horse was being tossed around upon the waves and the Amrun was our anchor.

The name that was emblazoned upon the radar was Ray Marine; I figured I would look up the meaning of all of the names of our party including this one when we got safely back to port. The interesting thing was I felt sure that we would all make it back to port. I knew that this journey had huge significance and that Spirit had our back. I felt the support from the hidden realms, not only were we, the crew, all playing our part, the mer-people were holding the boat afloat and the ancestors were with us every wave of our way.

When Mark overshot the radar yet again my attention switched from keeping Bobby safe to weaving strands of protection predominantly around both our captain and the wheel of the yacht. Everything happened in slow motion and I saw it happening before it did. The radar was behind the boat and Mark had let go of the wheel. He had positioned himself so he was at the edge of the stern hanging off a ladder. He reached out with his right arm and caught hold of the radar. I don't know how much the Ray Marine device weighs though I saw Bobby carry it later and I knew it was not light. It was also heavier because of the drag of the sea. I then saw exactly what Mark intended to do. His grip on the ladder was not as good as he wanted. He was looking to pull himself up to let go of the ladder completely so he could readjust his grip.

Bobby was still out on the starboard side of the bow, the wheel was unattended, the Wind Horse was rocking violently to the tempests beat and the captain was about to release any hold he had on the yacht. Everything had slowed down and the only thing I

knew to do was, in Mike's words, "Bring it on!" To be
the song, to be the threads and lines of support through
Amrun allowing Spirit to steer our vessel as they
steered mine and to wrap Mark in a protective web as
he looked to pull off this death-defying manoeuvre. If
he fell now we would not get him back.

It was though I was a witness throughout the whole
time that the boat and our lives were in peril, standing
and witnessing magic before my eyes. I do not have
the power to weave miracles, yet Spirit does, through
each of us, as we plug into the grid as hollow bones
and allow our hearts to be the rainbow threads of light,
we can transcend the greatest odds.

Mark was held by the strands of Amrun, by the
ancestors, by the mer-folk, and all of the invisible
realms as he let go of his hold. He was suspended for a
moment in time, in space, and then his hand sought out
and grabbed the rail. In forging a new grip, he pulled
the radar back aboard the Wind Horse. Bobby came

and carried it down into the cabin below and Mark shakily took control of the wheel.

The song continued to flow as the yacht stabilized and the mists cleared allowing Jamaica to once again come into view. The rain slowed and the waters were less threatening. Mark now had a visual guide from both the sight of land and buoys that were out in the sea. We were out of the storm and the threat to our lives had dissipated. As the last breath of Amrun was extinguished so the cold came to claim my bones. Before I descended into the cabin to dry off and thankfully borrow an oversized t-shirt from Mike, I pulled my phone from my pocket thinking to call Joyce. I wanted to hear her voice and let her know we were okay. Joyce is an empath and has a gift for sensing what is happening in the groups and within me when I am away from her working a medicine way. I had a strong inkling that she knew something big had happened on this journey to honour the ancestors. As I pressed the button to light up the screen it opened up on a text message that was ready to send to Joyce.

BEYOND STRANGE, BEYOND COINCIDENCE

As I stared at the screen of my phone a well of tears flowed from my heart to water my eyes. Looking up at me were two emojis. One was the face of an African baby and the other was of Caucasian hands in prayer. I understood the significance of these two images immediately, they were a gift from the ancestors. They were there to show their support, their gratitude, and the power of prayer. Before you move swiftly on from this piece I invite you to stop and marvel as I did. The first thing to note is that I had never used either one of these emojis before. I had seen the praying hands emoji as I have received it in correspondence from people on Facebook; however, I have not sent it or received it on my iPhone and I didn't know even a baby face emoji existed.

It was not until I returned home to Scotland that another piece fell into place for me. Although I was fully aware of the importance of these two images, one thing I had overlooked was that when you first choose a new emoji on an iPhone that involves a person, you get to choose the skin and hair colour. If I had known about the baby and looked for it to send to someone, or if I had gone to send the praying hands of gratitude, I would have chosen the milky white hands and a blonde haired pale baby face. I would have chosen images that match my own lily white "Celtic" skin tone and fair hair. These two icons had been selected through a process by Spirit. They had to have brought them up on my phone and then made their selection choosing the skin tones of the ancestors who were transported below decks from Africa and the British Isles and Ireland. I ask you, what other explanation is there? It was a part of the story that is beyond strange, beyond any trace of what some refer to as coincidence, it is Spirit talking through the veil in such a tangible way!

DRYING OFF

I am sure in part the adrenaline kept us warm, I know Spirit moving through me keeps me warm and once I knew we were safe and descended below deck I was freezing. Mike gave me a t-shirt with the sun god Lugh imprinted upon it. Lugh is connected to creativity, inspiration, hope, and vision. Mike is a larger framed man than me and as I was wringing out my soaking clothes in my dry new shirt, I thought about how much space had been created through our experience. A wry smile crept on my lips at the space I had inside of the t-shirt, space for more creativity, inspiration, and hope for a much bigger vision!

I was also struck by the fact that I never got sea-sick and that Pat had suspended her sickness when the maelstrom hit and went straight back to it once we were in safe waters. We had been sailing to have dinner at a restaurant on the beach, we never made that port and we never made dinner. We docked much later than anticipated and were driven the hour and a half straight back to Jackie's. I had a light breakfast and a hearty lunch. Pat, on the other hand, ended up offering her body as a sacrificial fast for the whole day!

It wasn't a calm sea that brought us back to port though it was a gentle one compared to what we had seen. In the first half of the day when we had returned I had been above deck in the sunshine, now I was with the ancestors as they had arrived in Jamaica — below deck. Though as we emerged and clambered up the steps to reach the sanctuary of dry land we were free. And in that freedom, there is a choice. Just as the boat was a hairs breath away from its tipping point, so are we as a species as a world. The tipping point is on the horizon and we have a choice to play a part whereby we will either capsize or navigate our way into a new world.

AN HONEST CAPTAIN

Mark drove us back to Jackie's and I sat beside him chatting about our experience. He shared that he has never before been in a sea or situation like we had encountered. He was grateful that no one panicked and was interested in the Amrun and the medicine way that carries me and others like me in the world. One thing that he said on the car ride brought another dimension to our journey. He openly and honestly admitted that the sail aboard the Wind Horse is too big for the boat. He told us how he has made several repairs because of this though nothing as dramatic as our adventure has ever happened before. When he gifted us this information instead of focusing on any negligence of the owner or on the fact the sail was too big for the boat, my mind went directly to the boat being too small.

A BIGGER BOAT

I went straight to the tapestry, to the medicine that was bursting forth from this incident-packed day. Of course, the sail was too big, for the boat was too small. If we are going to succeed in evolving as a species, we require a much bigger boat and a much bigger crew. Active participation from all aboard is essential, it is time to let go of the tag of passengers and step fully into the role of participants!

NAVIGATING A NEW WAY

I was struck by the importance of the radar being flung overboard and later the significance of retrieving it, though at the time the rational part of my brain had thought it was madness, as it screamed, "Let it be claimed by the sea!" However, my Spiritual bodies were in tune with the song of Amrun and again I reiterate I never once thought we would lose any of our crew, yet that rational voice did yell, "We could all die here!" It was important for me to get out of the way and let Spirit have the reins! I also think it helped significantly that I didn't understand sailing. A logical mind could have got stuck in fear and prevented the heart from being the driving force of change. Let that nugget sink in for a moment, for our heads will rebel at no longer having control. The logical mind looks to resist the patterns of change yet without change we will undoubtedly sink!

The aspect of the radar going overboard was important as I looked at the tapestry. The old ways, the patterns that we have looked to get ourselves out of the messes we have created do not work. It is time to release them overboard as we find new ways to bring our vessels into harbour, ways whereby we passionately partake in the evolution of the worlds. The mist that was created took us into the betwixt and between, a place where magic happens. In that mist, two black sailors risked their lives for the safety of four white passengers who in turn became active participants in keeping the sailors safe and the boat free from harm. The fact that two Jamaicans were in charge of the boat was not lost on me as we had sailed out that day. What a difference from the crews aboard ships that carried slave cargoes to these shores a couple of hundred years ago.

Our world is out of balance in so many ways: race discrimination, sexuality, war, religion, modern slavery, and pollution to name a few. Our pathway to evolution requires a paradigm shift, a new way to communicate with all beings seen and unseen. A way to honour all sentient beings, a heart way instead of a head way.

It may feel a bit rocky aboard a boat that we do not feel we are in control of. A boat that sails differently than what society has come to define as the acceptable and right way forward. This boat has Spirit at the wheel and it will take all of the crew doing what they know to do. We still need Captains and First Mates to bring their knowledge and wisdom of sailing to the party, just as we need those like Jenn who grew up on boats and know how to use a ship's/yacht radio to be there to communicate what is happening in the world and those like Mike who are willing to hold onto what will help us on our way and to let go of what no longer serves. And most assuredly it will require people like Pat and myself to let Spirit flow through us and activate a medicine way. It is the song of Spirit that will help us to transmute the fear, anger, and all of those attachments we have in the tangles of sorrow to be free through authentic joy that leads us to peace.

Why was bringing the radar back on board important? If we hadn't been focused on retrieving it, I may never have realised it had been flung overboard and I would have missed an important piece. I would also have missed seeing the name emblazoned upon its side and all names tell a story!

WHAT'S IN A NAME

I have always been interested in names for they all have meaning and carry vibrations within them. Our boat was named the Wind Horse — Mike had laughed at how well it was named for me with my last name being Steed. We certainly invoked the elements — we travelled on the sea powered by both the wind in her sails and the sun through green solar energy of the engine and the earth was represented by the horse which of course is a symbol of both travel and Sovereignty!

I looked up the names of the other major players that day. Those of us on board, the owner who drove us to the harbour, the name inscribed on the radar and Joyce who I had said would feel what was happening as far away as Scotland. I was right on that account, she was relieved to hear from me, she had been feeling things stirring big time from the moment we were celebrating singing "Redemption Song" until the time I called to share the adventure of our day.

Our Captain Mark is named after the god of war and it was certainly a transformational battle that took place on the high sea that day.

Bobby means bright and shining which is how the experience has left me, knowing that not only we can win this "RAW" and re-dream a new world, we have been shown a way to do so (which I will expand on shortly).

One meaning of Jennifer is white wave and we certainly rode those white horses to understand Sovereignty from a new perspective.

Michael means a gift from God and what a gift we have been given in finding a pathway that leads to evolution.

Pat means noble which means honest, uncorrupted, honourable, virtuous as well as high born and well-born. It seems to me that it is time for all of us to own the inner high queen and king in our own hearts and see all life as being high born rather than the old pattern of the aristocracy lording it over the masses.

Andrew means manly warrior, strong and brave; it is going to take us being all of these to reweave the outdated pattern on what it means to be a man. Are we willing to find the strength in sensitivity, the bravery to open our hearts and to get us out of both our genital head and the skull head?

Carolyn in one tradition is from the masculine Charles and means the feminine for manly. From my experience women, on the whole, have opened up their hearts so much more than the men have and I believe it is time for hearts to be opened even more fully so that the men can feel safe to come in and find strength in vulnerability to join those sisters who get the importance of being the vehicles of change. It is also important for women to feel safe and to release the old patterns of fear and anger that are often projected at men. It is time to fully awaken to releasing living in this Patriarchal world which is outdated, long in the tooth and does not work.

Another tradition lists Carolyn as being from Carol which means a song and dance of happiness. Of course it does! Spirit had all of this in hand — Amrun is a song and a dance that emanates authentic joy, freedom, and happiness.

Joyce is joyful and rejoicing. I am rejoicing in discovering this pathway to evolution is through authentic joy — my heart, my vessel, my soul runneth over.

Finally, we have Ray Marine the radar. Ray means wise protector and counsellor and Marine means from the sea. Who is the radar, the navigation system in the re-dreaming of the worlds? — Spirit.

What wiser counsellor can we have than Spirit? What better protector? The old communication system that we have used to find our way in the world is outdated, Spirit tossed it overboard so we could find a new way to navigate ourselves through the coming storms. As the radar was pulled from the sea I understood it to be a physical manifestation of this new pathway, a map that came from the edge of the world, a map that invites us to shift the salty tears of sorrow to salty tears of joy. It is important to spill our tears of sorrow so they are transmuted into tears of authentic joy. This is something I know how to do — it is something that other leaders in the healing community know how to do. The pathway to change is calling — it is time for our tears to blanket the Earth in joy! It is time to create a brave new world!

CHAPTER 5: A NEW WORLD

BEING THE DIFFERENCE

I received many nuggets of wisdom and confirmation from the work that transpired leading into and out of the zenith of what some call the Snow Moon, others the Hunger Moon, and the Storm Moon. I have seen both the February and March moon labelled as the Chaste Moon. There may be others too and I do enjoy delving into the meanings of names.

I had flown into Jamaica on the back of snow, sleet, and ice, I had experienced the storm of the Caribbean Sea, and Pat had taken on the role of fasting to arrive into port as the ancestors had with empty bellies and hunger upon them. As far as the aspect of chaste goes, the two meanings that jumped out for me in regards to this word are: simple and maiden.

The simplicity of it is we have choices to make. We can barrel along with a view that someone else will figure out the challenges ahead for us. This option smells of fear, apathy, and selfishness; alternatively, we can take responsibility and break out of the boxes and bubbles that have been our safety nets in this unsafe world. This means opening up our hearts and embracing a very different way of being in relation to the Earth and all of her inhabitants. It means to be present with our feelings and finding ways to live vibrantly in joy rather than exist behind masks tainted with sorrow.

This means embracing change which is outside of the comfort zone of many. I understand that creative types like myself are put into the "weirdo" bracket. I understand that we also live in a world where so many have trust issues. Yet surely now is the time to trust yourself to see, feel, hear, taste, and sense the world for what it is and what it can be. Are you able to glimpse that we are reaching our own tipping point? If so, then you will understand we have to choose which side of the boat to invest in. One that is chaotically heeling towards extinction or one that takes us to heeling into unknown territory and possible evolution.

I believe our choice is simple yet not easy. We have lived for so long in our heads that our pattern is to rationalise everything. I looked up the word *academia* and the English Oxford Living Dictionary describes its meaning as "the environment or community concerned with the pursuit of research, education, and scholarship." Yet our establishments look to dissect the world. We debate and argue over the smallest to the largest concepts through a head space, where logic and reason look to objectify ideas so we can box them up into the framework of our understanding.

I am at no point looking to leave our heads out of the equation, just as I am not looking to leave our gut out of it either. What though if we let go of leading from our head, what if we brought our gut and head space to meet our hearts and allowed this furnace, this fire, this symbol of love to be our guide. Are you willing to get in touch with your feelings and in so doing learn how to transmute all of your tangled strands of sorrow to joy?

What if the balance of our boat, our world, was addressed so that more beings become a living expression of authentic joy; can you visualise how this will create space and generate peace within and without? Are you willing to release your inner conflicts, doubts, and patterns of war so we can draw from a place of power? Do you have the courage to be a leader of heart or a follower of those who are holding clear space to meet you at the gateway of our hearts? Perhaps you are the one who will make the difference, your contribution will shift the worlds and I believe if you open your heart to be present with yourself and all beings you will be exactly that. All of us who do will be the difference!

MAIDEN

This indeed was a Maiden Moon in that it was the first moon of spring, a birthing moon with a birthing fire; it was an inaugural moment in time, for this marked a change in how I and those gathered would walk in the world from our involvement in this celebration.

In the "Celtic" world Brigid is the maiden, she heralds the coming of spring and this full moon marked the beginning of her season which is known both as Imbolc and Candlemas. I will return to the significance of Brigid's role in the 13-hour birthing fire in due course.

For now, let me begin by outlining some of the many 'aha' moments that took place during the gathering, from the small and what may seem inconsequential to those that were like a four by two knocking sense into us from Spirit.

I would like to reiterate the significance of the energetic connections to us from around the world everything had already magnified and those small treasures became bigger when the dots were connected in the tapestry.

IS ASTROLOGY A SCIENCE?

Joyce regularly sends information to me when I am working away regarding the significance of both new and full moons. You may think astrology, interpreting the movements of celestial bodies, the alignment of the planets, the movements of the sun and moon in relationship to humans is just a bunch of mumbo jumbo. I certainly think the horoscopes in daily tabloids can be considered too generic to be taken seriously. However, what I do know is that astrology has been a part of the fabric of the Universe for at least four thousand years. In our head world, astronomy has been accredited as a science whereas astrology is generally rejected by the scientific community as having no explanatory power for describing the Universe. There are most certainly strands of fear around astrology within some religious realms. Yet, perhaps dismissing astrology as being hocus pocus is a bit premature.

It is interesting to note that in some cultures these two practices were once united whereby astronomical data was used for astrological prognostication. It is also clear that many lay people seek out astrological teachings at holistic fairs as well as through the zodiac in newspapers, fortune tellers, psychic mediums, and the Chinese zodiac. There are certainly many charlatans in the world masquerading under the guise of being seers, manipulating and preying on people's curiosities. Yet there are many people who have genuine gifts and offer genuine insight that helps authentic seekers to grow. The point I am making is the argument of "there is no smoke without fire" works both ways here. It certainly casts a light on those who are disingenuous in working astrological ways and I totally accept that there are fraudsters out there. On the other hand, it also shines a light on those who through the ages have brought their gifts in service to help us mortals grow.

In the information Joyce sends me I have always looked at it as a combination of astrology and astronomy. In my world I know that there are forces bigger than myself and that the movement of the celestial world has an effect on human behaviour, I have certainly felt it and seen it. Take a full moon, how many of you have witnessed shifts in people? Just as the tides grow high so our emotions are stirred up.

ON POINT

What I also know is that each time Joyce sends me information during the waxing and waning of moon rises, it is exactly on point. It is always varied for the moon is in a different position with the planets, so obviously the information is for that conjunction, and each time what Spirit is already stirring within me and the group aligns with what comes through.

Here is what I received from Joyce as those gathered on the reef with me began our work. It was from an intuitive astrologer by the name of Tanaaz Chubb whose words you will see reflected everything that was stirring within and around us. As a side note, the name Tanaaz means — worthy of praise!

"On February 19th the full moon will be in the earth sign of Virgo. It will be a Super Moon, which means the moon will be closer to earth than on other occasions. It is going to be the strongest Super Moon of the year, which means that it will be at its closest point to the earth at this moment than it will be all year."

Virgo in the zodiac is an earth sign. This moon was offering us a chance to ground the medicine, to sew it into the fabric of the Earth so new shoots would grow from our work on the reef. The symbol of Virgo is a maiden carrying a shaft of wheat. In the "Celtic" culture we weave protective crosses that hang above our doors in this season. These crosses are woven from rushes and are known for Brigid — The Bride's Cross. I saw her plainly in both Virgo and the Maiden Moon

— extra confirmation of her presence with us!

"This moon will fall at zero degrees of Virgo. What makes this potent? — Zero — the number that is signified by a circle, one that is limitless with no beginning and no end. This number represents limitless possibilities. Zero is the blank canvas of all creation signalling that this moon is really going to offer infinite potential. It is going to help us realize our potential and the potential around us."

I had to read this piece several times to let it sink into my bones.

Spirit had aligned me with this moon of infinite potential to light a birthing fire to support the evolution of our species and the planet.

REALITY

"This moon will open us up, broaden our horizons, a transformational moon that will encourage us to open our minds and hearts. An opportunity to widen and deepen our perspectives beyond our current horizon, an opportunity to witness the world beyond our current reality."

I had felt this the moment that I had opened up this gathering to people around the world. All of the events leading up to this including the high sea adventure pointed to something of greater significance than I had so far dreamed. It was inviting us all to dream bigger, richer than we had ever dared dream before, with more vibrancy and in Technicolor. We had come to re-dream the worlds and Spirit had aligned the moon and planets to assist our work.

TRUST

"This moon calls us to trust that there is a higher purpose at work, that though life may be pulling us in different directions and challenges are at our door, our experiences are here to lift us higher and with our hearts open we will grow. What the human mind may see as horrifying or abrasive our soul may be rejoicing in the teachings we receive with the depth of emotion and life-changing wisdom that is obtained. Looking through a Spirit lens affords us a new perspective that transcends our egos."

With each line read, I felt the importance of the teachings I had received on the high sea. For some that journey would have been horrifying, it was certainly abrasive as I clung onto the rail for dear life as we were heeling! All of this had prepared me for the life-changing wisdom that was percolating within me. I felt Spirit's hand in bringing us all together in a clearer way than I/we have ever seen before. I felt my knowing going deeper and with it the understanding that the people in circle with me were receiving the teachings in a much richer way than I have provided before. And there was that word again — Trust. What if each of us has a higher purpose? What if we trusted Spirit to lead us to a higher purpose? What if we dared to imagine? — Perhaps prophets like John Lennon have been paving a way to our greatness all along!

RELEASE

"The light of this full moon is going to be so strong, its energy so intense that we will instinctively open our hearts. Our life stories will be released and exposed, we will be cut open so we can see the authentic truth of what bubbles at our core. This exposure and release can happen on a physical, mental, and spiritual level or a combination of all three. Especially poignant will be the release of the old patterns of repetitive thoughts, the stress of worry, and fears of our future."

This is exactly what we were on the reef to work with. To be a hollow bone so we could serve Spirit and sing home the displaced/lost souls and energise the Dragon Lines. This meant beginning with "healer heal thyself" and flushing our own bodies. By creating space within these bodies we would expand the space for Spirit to work through us. It always begins with personal healing so we can vibrate at a higher frequency for planetary healing. I had planned major release work over the first couple of days including a powerful birthing ceremony for each of us to cleanse and prepare before we would sing home the souls and work the collective birthing at the all-night fire.

I recognised the importance of letting go of all doubts and fears around the enormity of our task in re-dreaming the world. If we stayed in the appearance of how the world will view the visions that I had received from a headspace, then the walls of doubt would box us in. We had to let go of the worry that we may fail and step into being the medicine regardless. It is powerful to move forward with certainty that *"we can"* in our hearts. Whether we will or not is beyond my individual control and the control of those who had gathered with me.

ONE HUNDRED PERCENT

I know that collectively homo sapiens have a chance to support the evolution of the worlds, that knowledge is enough for me to bring my 100% to the party. I am willing and prepared to give it my all, are you?

I invited each of us at the gathering to give 100%, no more, no less. I always look to meet people where they are at and I know that each of us are on different journeys and are at different places, yet 100% remains 100%.

I spoke to my personal trainer about this recently. When I go to the gym I give my all, I look to give my all in everything I do. He was sharing how he loves training people like me because we give everything to the process, that we understand that we are competing solely with ourselves. When we get into comparing and competing against others in the gym then ego is in our way. I shared how when I work in schools with youth that I ask them to grade themselves — their own grade is more important than the teachers. Not all see it that way as the teacher's grade is what counts academically. Yet we all know when we earn our 'A' rather than are given it. A student who gets the 'A' easily and yet is disruptive and lazy knows full well that they have not put in the effort to deserve that 'A'. On the other hand, a student who gets a conventional C+ and has given a 100% has grafted for their 'A'. Where a conventional 'A' student excels in my book, is in the support that they offer to those around them, how they help others to be better than their conventional grades.

My challenge to each of us at the gathering was to bring our 'A' game, our 100% so we could all grow exponentially. I was to reiterate this at the 13-hour fire stating that I would prefer people offered one hour by the fire at 100% rather than hanging out all night offering sporadic energy and sucking from the fire. When people do this it makes my job much harder.

I have led all night gatherings before and this was the first one where I would be plugging into the song of Spirit with Amrun with a group for such an extended period of time. I was excited about it and I had an inner knowing that Spirit would carry the song vibrantly through me as I have spent years building the muscle to be such a vessel. All that I had planned would prepare each of us to offer a bigger 100% than we had ever given before.

GRANDEST DREAM

Tanaaz's words continued to hit home:

"This moon will bring our core fears to the surface, it will agitate some of our beliefs to bring awareness and exposure to them. Most of us have fear lurking in the corner of our minds and hearts and, while this is part of the human experience, the more conscious we can become of our fear, the more it helps us to know when it is driving our decision or when it is simply in the background as a way to protect us. Fear can be healthy in reasonable doses, yet most of us are over-

driven with fear, which keeps us stuck in repetitive patterns and a lower vibrational state.

On this Full Moon, work on becoming aware of your fears. Acknowledge them. Stand them down. Pierce them with your gaze straight to the core, for doing so will loosen their grip on your life. Sometimes, all you have to do is become aware of where you are operating with fear and the rest will follow."

What was being asked of us was to look our fears squarely in the face. Fear is a natural part of all our lives; when we worry we use lower vibrational energy, incessant worries that wrap cords of fear around our past and our future binds us to a lower vibrational force. I marvelled at the next piece relating to our fears:

"The Universe is calling you to release the fears of bondage to earthly illusions. On the flip side of fear is your grandest dream. Your fears are not to be ignored, rather they are there to be challenged. Rise up to them,

for you are strong enough, and the power of this moon will be helping you."

What was my grandest dream? — **The evolution of our species and planet.**
This moon was a birthing and we were the midwives, it was a new beginning into the dawn of expanded consciousness. I realised my fears were wrapped around being able to increase the luminosity of my flame so it can be seen in the world, with so many doubters, so many people ready to slay the dragon, to dismiss a pathway that seems abstract, strange, outside of their framework of reference, it takes courage to stand in one's light of truth. I sensed the enormity of what Spirit was asking of me. A part of me recognised and relished the opportunity to stand in the frontline of this "RAW" and part of me felt overwhelmed. The illusion of running out of time, figuring a way to share this information with the world, the challenges of getting this information out to the masses, having people look outside of their comfort zones felt heavy and yet on the flip side I felt a lightness of Spirit in the

knowledge that "we can!"

I have always felt that I was born onto the planet at this moment in time to meet the darkness gripping our world and illuminate it with my light. To join my heart with the hearts of all of the other beings who were also brought to this space and time for the same reason - the evolution of the worlds. I wonder how many of you reading this resonate deeply with this cosmology? For those that don't, I hope you look to those that do for guidance. What have you got to lose? — Possibly everything if you don't.

SELF CARE

The writings of Tanaaz that Joyce shared continued:

"Self-care is always so important and on this full moon we really have to pay attention and look after our physical bodies as much as possible. A huge part of this is also practising self-love, and accepting our bodies no matter what, even if we are faced with illness or disease."

Seeing ourselves clearly and loving ourselves authentically regardless of earthly illusions plugs us into the light of Spirit. Spirit shines so radiantly within each and every being. Through self-love, we radiate joy and love in its purest form. What if we build the muscle to hold this charge in our bodies? Surely we will hold space for ourselves and all other beings to evolve. I know there are many people out there who have awakened to this heart thought and many others who are on the fence. My hope is that enough of us will step forward and through being present with ourselves and all sentient beings that we will activate a major shift. What if we encourage the doubters to get into their bodies and be present with themselves and all life? As we banish the doubt and replace it with love we edge closer to a new tipping point. What if enough of us embrace the change? I believe it will open up spaces inside of us that allow us to access so far untapped knowledge and wisdom which will in effect lead the planet and all of us beings into evolution. The great news is that I believe it will carry all of the doubters with us.

Again I reiterate that the simple decision for each of us to make is — **Will we wage WAR or RAW in these uncertain times?**

Will we cling to old ideals that sink our ship, stand on the side-lines (sit on the fence) immobilised in fear and be swept overboard or will we embrace a new reality and be an active participant in change?

OTHER WORLDS

This moon was all about cracking us open whether we know it or not for the seeds of change to take root within us. As I read Tanaaz's words all that was stirring for the gathering made complete sense. I felt the shifts already taking place in my own bodies. The final words talked of the mer-people and the dragons, of worlds connected to our world:

"We perceive reality to be a solid, three-dimensional world, yet for those who have expanded their mind and awareness, it is easy to see there are dimensions beyond this, life beyond this, and realms beyond this. Life is not what we see, there is an unseen world too, and if you open to the Moon's energy, if you allow it to shine straight through your soul, you will be able to awaken this awareness and see that life can be imagined and lived in far more detail, in far more vivid colour, and with far more magic."

What if our world affects other worlds? I don't know whether you even believe in the existence of other worlds though as I have already shared they are as natural to me as the sun and moon are in ours. The unseen worlds are sometimes seen by visionaries and those whose hearts expand to wander between the veil. There are those amongst us on this planet who claim that planet Earth/planet water is not their original home. That many worlds are connected and portals are open from their worlds to ours. Some who know that they have come to the planet at this moment in time, when space is at such a premium, to help create the space for the birthing of the worlds. What if in evolving as a species the portals to other worlds open? What if by emanating authentic joy we help heal not only ourselves and this planet, we support the unfolding of an evolutionary Universe?

Why not dream big? Why not re-dream the most creative expression of Oneness? As I have said I do not know what the final picture looks like, probably because nothing can ever be fixed, there is no final picture. Yet I feel the expansion of space within me, created through the release of old patterns.

What if we all committed to walking through our fear of the unknown and chose to vibrate at a higher frequency? Surely you are able to glimpse the possibility of reaching a different kind of tipping point? I hope so, for without you we may fall short and perhaps like those in the Lost City of Atlantis, we will see the dream fade into darkness and so begin again. Whichever way we go, extinction or evolution I do not see it as an end, it will be a new beginning yet one way will swallow us up in the strand of sorrow and one will pluck us on the strand of peace.

I read all of this information Joyce sent several times through the gathering to let the enormity of Tanaaz's words sink fully into our bones.
Another piece came through the following morning.

THE NEW WORLD?

I had awoken before sunrise and I had wandered down to sit close to the breaking surf and watch night become day. I love the gloaming, the betwixt and between space of both a morning sunrise and an evening sunset. The moon was still in the sky growing full by the hour and the sun peeked through orange rays painting the sky in shades of pink and blue.

I watched a pair of herons scavenging the rocks for food when I heard the voice of Bobby in my mind singing, *"Christopher Columbus is a damn blasted liar."* I was then struck by the masquerade of the world. Columbus is credited with the discovery of the New World; many boats then sailed to the New World where on the back of genocide, the subjugation of indigenous people and the slave trade, new countries were formed. This was achieved through the dominating nature of the Europeans as they brought their beliefs and customs to live their lives into their New World. Some states in the USA still have a federal holiday marking Columbus' discovery — a sailing route to the Americas. He is recognised in history for discovering the New World, a continent that was not known to the Old World. A continent that was teeming with life, where you could drink the water straight from the streams, with fish and animals aplenty, large forests and wide open spaces. In five hundred years the New World has been contaminated by the Old World. The animals are disappearing at an accelerated rate of knots, drinking water directly from streams is no longer commonplace, the Island of New York is now a concrete jungle and space is a premium.

I never understood why intelligent people would buy
into such nonsense of Columbus' so-called discovery
when as Burning Spear rightly asks, "What about the
Arawak Indians?" Indigenous people overlooked as
the Europeans claimed dominion over the land.

As I sat there on this morning I perceived this story in
a new way. It wasn't a revolutionary way, it was a
minor shift and yet it provided a major one in the
tapestry — A New World. The so-called New World
of Columbus' fabrication was never a new world, all
that happened was the Europeans brought their ideas
and values of dominion and recreated an old pattern of
discrimination and religious intolerance.

The pilgrims who were Puritans first settled in the
USA after their voyage on the Mayflower. They had
fled England because of religious persecution yet
brought their own bigotry with them. They cried a
right for freedom to pray in their own way yet denied
others the right to do the same. Those that did not
kowtow to those who held the greatest influence in

developing the patterns in the New World were banished, put to death or beaten into submission.

Those that left the Old World replicated a pattern. Through religion and the armed forces, a version of the world that has been part of the fabric of history for eons was recreated. A world built on the premise of freedom yet, in reality, it was built on the pillars of church and state — religious dogma and war.

A NEW WORLD

What I heard from Spirit that morning is, **"It is time to create a New World."** It is time to release the doctrine that has bound us to religious malpractices and embrace the heart of all religious teachings which is — **love**. It is time to release the old world and embrace a new world.

CHAPTER 6: THREADS WITHIN THE TAPESTRY OF CHANGE

JAMAICA: A BRIEF OVERVIEW

The Saladoid culture flourished in this land from 500 BCE until being absorbed by the Taino/Arawak people who also came from Venezuela.

The name Yamaye — Xaymaca — and later Jamaica means land of wood and water. Jamaica was once even more densely forested than its current state, which still covers close to a third of the land mass. Yet, like so many other lands, the coverage is on a decline rather than an incline. With a cloak of trees, one hundred and twenty rivers, and the sea greeting all sides of the land, it is well named.

In researching pieces of its story I revelled in discovering the names of both a Taino god and goddess. To speak their names on the wind was such a blessing — a way to remember and honour the ancestors of this land.

Imagine finding the names of your ancestors from five hundred plus years ago, if you are fortunate to have done so, then like me, I am sure it gave you a thrill and a deep connection to your roots. Speaking my ancestors' names on the wind is empowering.

And so it was for me to speak the names of a god and goddess, connected beyond family lines, to a collective consciousness of those who had gone before. It deepened the connection with the ancestors in a clear way and I believe helped gather even more support in the invisible realms for the work we were doing.

Yúcahu, son of Atabey, is associated with the spirit of cassava; cassava is a crop akin to yucca, and he also has associations with the sea.

Atabey, the mother of Yúcahu, is a goddess of fresh water and fertility. As I have shared, names carry power — the remembrance of a goddess and god whose names were once regularly spoken with respect and love was deeply enriching.

To add to the celebration of those who have gone before, I was able to add a third name to honour all of those who still live in the heart of this land, I was gifted the name of Nyankipong to place on the wind. This is the Maroons name for almighty God! The Maroons were birthed out of the slave trade that came to this land with the arrival of the Spanish occupation.

Xaymaca came under Spanish rule in 1494 CE after Columbus sailed to these shores. The influx of Europeans brought deathly disease to the majority of the indigenous people. Alongside the new immigrants, slaves were introduced to work the land for the new masters that had displaced the Taino. This created an unexpected new culture on the island, for the slaves that escaped fled into the mountains banded together and formed a new tribe. These refugee communities hid in the forested mountains comprising of any surviving indigenous people along with escaped slaves. They took on the name — Maroons; I have heard a couple of different meanings for this name, one being "escaped slaves" and another "mighty friend." What is clear is that the Maroons have left their mark on the story of this land.

When the Spanish abandoned their plantations after ceding "ownership" of Jamaica to the English forces, many of the slaves took to the mountains to join the Maroons.

Scotland also had its hands in the blood of the slave trade. The financial profits of tobacco and sugar made some families rich on the backs of those who were shackled in slavery and servitude. In 1796, thirty per cent of Jamaican estates were owned by Scots, in 1817 it had risen to thirty-two per cent. As I have alluded to earlier, my lineage through my grandmother's side of the family, her father's family, respected lairds, part of the gentry of Scotland, made their fortune through slavery. My work in Jamaica has been guided by Spirit all along through unravelling the knots, breaking the chains, creating freedom and space for the ancestors which include my direct lineage.

I totally get why our ancestors have fought wars against oppression in traditional ways. I admire the Maroons who took back their liberty albeit in fighting two guerrilla wars against the British. Their invisibility in the mountains of Jamaica served them well as the British failed in their attempts to track them. Little wonder really for the Maroons were and are a hardy people. They had to be to survive and thrive in this new land that was now home. There were no roads into the mountains which thwarted any British pursuit. To access the Maroon settlements, you would have needed to follow the river's course and then attempt a hazardous climb via vines growing down from waterfalls!

The wars fought by the Maroons brought them a legal recognition of their autonomy and freedom. They won their liberty in the 1700s, decades prior to the British abolishing the slave trade in 1833 and over two-hundred years before Jamaica received independence from the British Crown.

To this day there is a State Nation within this Island Nation. Nestled high in the mountains on the western side of Jamaica in St. Elizabeth is the settlement of Accompong. Traditional life abounds here, the customs and ways of the modern day Maroons connect deeply with their ancestral roots in a thriving and trusting community.

Times call for us to transform wounded wastelands into thriving realms where we can trust each other unequivocally. A time for us to be "Mighty Friends" to all beings and for new patterns to be woven into the tapestry. Patterns where people stand strong and stand against the forces that will look to sweep us aside. Patterns of RAW!

How we communicate with ourselves, others and the planet are of paramount importance. I will speak on the power of thoughts and the vibrational impact of them shortly; before I do I would like to expand on Brigid whose season we were in according to the "Celtic" calendar and how her connections with my homeland were woven into the work that was unfolding on the reef.

I was delighted to learn about a communication device that is still in operation today amongst the Maroon community — the Abeng. The Abeng is a cow horn that was used as a war horn during times of conflict and now in times of peace it is used as an instrument akin to the modern day cell phone, a way for the tribe to speak to each other over long distances. It is said that the sound of the horn can be heard over 15 kilometres/9 plus miles away.

BRIGID AND THE ABENG

It was with glee that I connected the dots of a medicine way. Both Brigid as the Christian Saint and Pagan Goddess are associated with the cow. There is a stone carving on St. Michael's church tower on the top of Glastonbury Tor in Somerset, England, that depicts St. Brigid with her cow. The cow in the "Celtic" culture is a symbol of abundance. Stories of St. Brigid abound with tales of her travelling with a white cow with red ears that gave a never-ending supply of milk. Milk is the poetry of life, the first drink that we humans taste on the planet.

I have a beautifully carved cow horn that I work with in ceremony. Instead of the tip being cut to make a sound, it is fully intact. The tip has been intricately carved into the shape of an acorn. It resembles the head of a penis. Along its length, engraved into this dermal bone, is an oak tree with sprouting leaves and a Pictish Boar, it is an open container, a vessel that I work with in making offerings to the land and to the waters. This opening represents the sacred feminine, the vagina. This vessel's structure, shape, and adornments mark it as being both masculine and feminine. Interestingly horns grow on both cows and steers/bulls. Abengs are naturally connected to the sacred feminine and masculine!

I brought the cow horn to Jamaica, an Abeng, as a device to communicate in peace and RAW! At the opening ceremony it was filled with offerings of rum, waters from around the world that each of us had carried with us and our spit, our DNA. Our spit carried our oaths to serve all beings for the highest good, to be present with ourselves so we could connect deeply with the land of wood and water and all beings seen and unseen! Offerings from the Abeng were placed into the earth as we gathered in a small grove of trees and also into the sea as we blessed the waters.

Along with the names of Yúcahu, Atabey, and Nyankipong, I added the names of those who are remembered in the stories of the "Celtic" lands including Brigid. She is known as the Foster Mother and Godmother to Christ, an Aid-Woman to Mary, and a Midwife who births the light.

How important it is to gather the highest vibration of light to walk into the shadows of our past and of our present to effect change in our present and our future. If we get stuck in the patterns of our past, we can easily fall into victimhood and hopelessness. War has gripped us in its claws driving our belief of reality. This excerpt from Bernard Cornwell's account of how England became governed under one King in his series on Alfred the Great in the 9th Century CE is a clear example. This one sentence plainly describes both the patriarchal world and our entrenchment in the pattern of hopelessness:

"There has always been war and there will always be war. So long as one man wants another man's wife, or another man's land, or another man's cattle, or another man's silver, so long will there be war. And so long as one priest preaches that his god is the only god or the better god there will be war."

RAW offers us an alternative where "WE CAN" if we will. It will take a leap of faith away from the ingrained concept of our current collective consciousness. As we face the darkness that looks to eclipse our world surely it is time to embrace all of the support that transcends religious dogma so we can birth light into the lives of all beings seen and unseen.

BRIGID

I was here to celebrate the coming of Brigid's season, to align with the natural world and meet her in an old ancestral way under the light of the moon. All of the four "Celtic" seasons, Imbolc (Spring), Beltane (Summer), Lughnasadh (Autumn) and Samhain (Winter) are fire festivals. Celebrating these fire festivals are ways to connect an earthly fire with the strength of the sun. Working under the light of the moon at these liminal times connects the sun and moon energies, the masculine and feminine, the fire and the waters. Lighting an all-night fire on the reef by the Caribbean Sea under the Imbolc full moon had brought the birthing powers of Brigid with me!

EXPLORING THREADS OF BRIGID WITHIN THE TAPESTRY

As stated, when leading retreats, the energy instantly magnifies, the tapestry is revealed more clearly because we are a microcosm of the macrocosm. As our taxi driver Franklin drove Pat and I through the pouring rain on the day of our arrival, I reflected on the fact that my suitcase had arrived soaking wet.

I had picked up my bag from the conveyor belt to find it drenched with water. I had unzipped it and shoved my hand in to feel damp clothes inside. I have a soft suitcase and the water had seeped through.

In all my years of travel, it was the first time I had collected a drenched bag and I pondered the significance. My thoughts went immediately to Brigid.

I had flown to Jamaica with the Brigid Flame. As a saint, she founded a double monastery in Kildare around 480 CE for both men and women. She was a powerhouse of a woman who in a Patriarchal age left an impression throughout Ireland and the whole of the British Isles. As a goddess she is also linked with fire and water, her father the Dagda has three daughters all named Brigid, a triple goddess of healing, smith craft, and poetry.

As the Brigidine Sisters of Kildare will tell you, a sacred fire burned in this small Irish town reaching way back into pre-Christian times. Scholars suggest that priestesses tended an eternal flame invoking the triple goddess Brigid to protect their herds and to provide a fruitful harvest.

Brigid has strong links to both paganism and Christianity. As the saint, she is said to have continued to tend this eternal fire with nineteen nuns to aid her. When she died the tradition continued. In the twelfth century, a Welsh Chronicler Gerald of Wales reported that the fire was still burning. It is thought that it was extinguished in the sixteenth century during the suppression of the monasteries.

RELIGHTING THE FLAME

The Brigidine Sisters are a restoration of the ancient fifth century Order of St. Brigid of Kildare. They were established by Bishop Daniel Delany in Tullow, County Carlow Ireland on February 1st, 1807. In 1992 a group of Brigidine Sisters moved to Kildare to connect with their Celtic roots and to reclaim Brigid of Kildare in a new way for a new millennium. In 1993 they re-lit the Brigid Flame and from that day to this, the Brigidine Sisters have tended the perpetual flame. It now resides in Solas Bhride, a Christian Spirituality Centre that focuses on St. Brigid and the early Christian Celtic tradition.

The Brigidine Sisters tend this flame honouring the divine in everyone and everything.

BALANCE OF FEMININE AND MASCULINE

So, of course, she was with me — I was carrying a candle lit from the Brigid flame of Kildare! The candle also carried the flame from the Dalia Lama's Peace Candle that was lit at the turn of the Millennium as a beacon for world peace.

The 13-hour Full Moon Imbolc Birthing Fire was going to be lit from a candle blessed by these two lights. A sacred balance of the divine feminine and masculine that carries the energies connected to these two flames. This united flame would light our way through the darkness of the night into the dawn and daylight culminating with the zenith of the full moon.

I reflected on all of the people connected to these two flames. The hundreds of thousands who have lit candles from these fires and whose prayers have been spoken or thought as they have burned brightly in their homes and at gatherings throughout the world. In association, they would also be connected albeit subconsciously through the ethers. I wondered what the impact would be, how this would amplify the magic!

Yet I am sure you are wondering what on earth this has to do with my wet bag?

My reflections on my soaked suitcase centred around Brigid and the breaking of the waters. It is said that Brigid dips her fingers and melts the ice upon the waters allowing them to flow as winter gives way to spring.

Just as a mother's waters break heralding the arrival of a child, the land mirrors this in the seasons of our lives. Spring our infancy a time of rebirth, summer our adolescence where the green world explodes and colours abound, autumn our adulthood where we reap the harvest with the fruits of our labour, and winter our elder years, a quietening time of reflection, integration, and restoration.

MIDWIFE

In the "Celtic" tradition Brigid as the midwife offers us an opportunity to reflect on what it is we will birth during this season of Imbolc. The full moon, the Maiden Moon, symbolised the pregnancy and birthing of the season and our prayers and visions that had been collected were going to be energised by all of the strands that had brought this gathering together.

The thought of the breaking of a mother's waters in preparation for the birthing to begin was not lost on me. Inside my soaked suitcase was the drum that would sing its song on the reef. Its heartbeat would echo into the ethers as we worked a medicine way on the highest good of all beings. This blessing of water was an auspicious start!

Not only was my bag wet, but the heavens also opened and were blessed with a torrential downpour that lasted from the moment we climbed into the taxi until we reached Negril and Jackie's on the Reef. In my three visits to Jamaica, all at the same time of year, I had not witnessed such rain, the intensity of it, the length that it fell for and that it was during the daytime and not in the evening/wee hours before dawn was a new one for me.

The song of the Universe that presented itself to me on arrival was all about the waters. From the rain that fell from the skies to the waves that crashed splendidly upon the reef. Water was asking to be heard. I had witnessed the sea foam spraying over the salt water pool and the dock at Jackie's in previous years, yet this was more dramatic, far more intense.

I had pondered how I was going to dry my clothes, any sunshine was a day away, even if the rain stopped it was cloudy with a cool dampness in the air. You can imagine my surprise and delight to find that my clothes were no longer damp when I opened my suitcase. Perhaps if they had been I could have dried them because the rain made way for strong winds that night and continued throughout the next day.

I was grateful for the protective screen that was lowered over the half-moon window that looked out onto the sea that night. The difference in temperature inside the dome was felt immediately. It also allowed me to light the candle with the Brigid Flame and Peace Candle that was on my altar and from this flame I lit nightlights that were perched on stones jutting out from the wall. I felt such peace in my heart and revelled in the magic that was flowing within me and around me as I drifted into the dreamtime in this sanctuary that was my home for the next ten days.

CHAPTER 7: PLUCKING THE THREE STRANDS OF POETRY

DEATH ON THE REEF

As Pat and I had sat in the taxi on our way to Jackie's, we ended up following a funeral car. Again, I was cognisant of the little signs that were coming in from the Universe. We followed death and then overtook the funeral car on the final stretch of road leading to the retreat centre and my thoughts turned to rebirth. For only when death is fully realised can new life flourish.

The name of the car left an impression too. It was a Toyota with the name of Noah. I have not seen a model of a car named Noah before. My thoughts drifted to the biblical story of the ark, a tale of a great cleansing through mass flooding and the rebirthing of the world as the animals went in and out of the ark two by two. A high king and queen of all of the animals that were saved from the floods for the rebirthing of the world.

During dinner that night, Jackie shared that the funeral car had been going to the hotel next door to hers. A woman had drowned there earlier in the day. Jackie knew her, she was an experienced diving instructor who often came to Jackie's and swam in the sea off of Jackie's dock. She had not come to Jackie's that day for she knew Jackie would have refused to allow her to enter such forceful waters. I listened to the version of the story that was told to me in regards to this woman's drowning. Apparently, she had coerced a student to join her. Her student was reluctant though he had finally agreed to enter and was fortunate to clamber out again. She, on the other hand, had been slammed against the reef and consequently drowned.

Again, I looked for the significance of what the Universe was gifting through the story. I knew that all of these happenings tied into a much bigger picture of our healing journey in Jamaica.

Her name was Martina, and again we return to the meaning of names. Martina is the feminine version of Martin which, like Mark (our captain on the yacht), is derived from the Roman god of war Mars. So here we had a death of war to greet our arrival. This carried huge significance as we gathered for a retreat that would explore the difference between being in sovereignty with the land and all beings and living in dominion over others and the planet. It cried of a different song to be woven on the wind, to go into battle in a very different way, to RAW. The old patterns of war will die or we will be consumed by them as we have been for eons, a failure to grasp a new way of being will most assuredly lead to the elimination of our species.

We were also in Jamaica to sing home lost and displaced souls. Martina's actions in looking to impose her way of mastering the elements and swimming in such a dangerous sea and her subsequent death were a microcosm of the macrocosm. She was to become unwittingly a sacred offering, a sacrifice, to mirror homo sapiens rampage of war and dominion that is currently rife throughout the planet.

As Jackie rightly said during our meal, Martina died doing what she loved, that in itself is a blessing. I knew that we would honour her death by singing her home in case she was stuck in the void.

After our boat ride on the high sea, I reflected that our Captain, First Mate, Mike, and Jenn all have a love for sailing; Pat and I could have gone down with them and the vessel with Amrun singing in our bones and we would all have met death that day loving what we were doing. However, we didn't die. We never were in danger of dying for Spirit wanted this tale to be told. Spirit is speaking through us and calling us to create space so life can flow abundantly within us and around us.

My thoughts went to her student and I wondered how he would process his day. Would he shift into gratitude for his life? Would he learn to trust his own voice that had obviously screamed, *"Do not go into the water!"* and say no next time he faced such a huge dilemma? Or would he react to this day and spend years drowning in the strands of PTSD, anger, grief, or even guilt? It is amazing how many survivors of tragedies end up feeling guilty that they survived and others didn't. I pondered how many beings who witnessed the event were caught in the threads of sorrow and how this magnified represented the millions who are wrapped in cords that drown them, again and again, each day.

He represented the people of the world who follow the leaders, the experts that so often take us into their web of how things need to be done. We are like this man — we now stand on the edge of a momentous storm that looks to drown us all, will we continually follow leaders who place dominion over the planet ahead of sovereignty and dive in behind? Or will we do things differently and look to leaders of heart to pluck the strands of poetry and lead us into a new dawn?

A VIOLENT WORLD

There is no getting around the fact that violence on mass has been and still is part of our world's story. Jamaica's story reflects this and according to United Nations estimates for many years now, has one of the highest murder rates in the world. Statistics show that crime is high and intolerance deep-rooted — a vicious homophobic culture exists spilling over into horrendous killings that perpetuate fear rather than freedom.

WHEN NON-INDIGENOUS MEETS INDIGENOUS

Jamaica's bloody past, which includes the elimination of the indigenous ancestors through contact with non-indigenous diseases, extends beyond the decimation of human life to encompass the destruction of many other beings.

Snakes are extremely rare on the Island having been killed off mostly by the introduction of the mongoose. Why was the mongoose brought to Jamaica? Homo sapiens wanted to protect profits. Sugar plantations were losing money so mongoose were imported to kill off cane-field rats.

The major flaw here is that in introducing the mongoose Jamaica brought an animal into an environment free of mammal predators. With no beings hunting the mongoose, it has resulted in an ecosystem disaster. This human desire to create profit and claim dominion over the land has drastically impacted the populations of snakes, lizards, ground-nesting birds, and sea turtles putting them on the threatened or endangered species list!

This is not solely a Jamaica story, there are countless tales of plants, humans, and other animals being introduced to countless other lands that have severely impacted natives' populations. One such example is the decimation of the red squirrel through the introduction of the grey squirrel in the British Isles.

Just as human souls can get stuck in limbo because the death of their physical bodies remains unprocessed, so do other beings. All sentient beings are impacted by the way they die. For our animal, vegetable, and mineral kingdoms the exploitation and abusive treatment of these beings have led to more strands of sorrow staining the land resulting in more unprocessed deaths and souls to be sung home.

CREATING SPACE

Witnessing the elements in their fullness from my arrival with a day of persistent rain, to one of blustery wind, to the boat ride that began in bright sunshine and then encompassed all of the elements in their keenest before the sailboat finally brought us safely back to land. I certainly felt the energies of the elements stirring within me and around me.

The importance of creating space in our own bodies, of purifying and cleansing our own bodies so we could expand space for Spirit to work through us as hollow bones was exactly what I had on the cards.

Behind Jackie's retreat centre is her organic gardens where her staff team tend fruits and vegetables that are harvested for the meals that are lovingly prepared by Gwen and Vanetta with the help of Nick, the three kitchen staff who provide such wonderful support to fuel our bodies as we stir the cauldron of change in our work.

Behind the garden is a cave which I love to descend into to weave with the three Strands of Poetry.

THREE STRANDS OF POETRY

I came across the story of the Dagda's Harp many years ago; what I have enjoyed about my time with the stories of my "Celtic" ancestors is finding a blueprint of a medicine way in the folds of the story. I have written about this extensively in my book *Magical*

Crows, Ravens, and the Celebration of Death. I would like to give a brief overview here for those who have not read this work and are unfamiliar with this medicine way.

"In the stories the harp has magical properties; it brings the seasons into order, it prepares one to go into battle, and it plucks the three strands of poetry."

Let's stop a moment and reflect on this. It is so easy to see that our seasons right now are out of order. It is clear that we are in the greatest battle homo sapiens have ever faced as we edge closer to the tipping point of extinction for so many species including our own. What if we could pluck the harp and put the seasons back into order? The good news here is we can.

When we open up to creatively experience ourselves as the Dagda's Harp we can pluck the three magical strands associated with it. These three strands are named sorrow, joy, and peace. We are all too familiar with plucking the strand of sorrow, our planet is immersed in singing this song with all of the attributes that I have listed under the umbrella of the sorrow strand.

What Spirit guided me to was a way to work with the harp to transmute suffering. I begin by keening, which means to wail, to cry, not crocodile tears, real genuine sorrow. Through the vibration of the sounds that come through me, I release the sorrow and all the aspects under the umbrella of this strand from my bodies. This can be intense and scary for it is real. There are so many layers of tangled knots that people have suppressed in their bodies. It is scary to meet ourselves, to own our own sh-t. Yet when we are willing we can transform our sh-t into fertiliser. I strongly recommend seeking out someone who can hold clear space for you to enter this medicine gateway. This is powerful medicine and the last thing you are looking for is to get stuck in the sorrow or spin out with it all and create more chaos. For if we enter this process and fail to transmute the sorrow we dump ours out of our vessel and puke it up all over the land.

On our first full day on the reef, I led the group
through the three strands. In the release of sorrow, you
may find that you retch, possibly puke, and most likely
spit up phlegm. I begin the song of sorrow using the
name of the Dagda's Harp Uaithne (Oo-en-ya). I wail
these three syllables over and over again extinguishing
the strands of sorrow that are in my bodies.

It is a practice that I return to regularly for when I keen
some of the strands are my own sorrows and others
tangles are from what I have picked up from other
beings. The more empathic we are the more we ingest
from others. We are all porous beings and simply
walking through an enclosed space that is full of
people will result in spillages of energy from one to
another. Thoughts, as well as actions, have a vibration,
they go somewhere and some splatter into other
people's bodies!

What I always advocate is only release what your
bodies are ready to release on this day. At no point do
we look to the story of what the "sorrow" is, this is not

about dredging up our past and sitting in the tangled threads of our story whereby we can get stuck and they strangle us. It is about allowing the strand of sorrow to flow through you until you have plucked all that you can in that given moment. Here is where a bridge occurs, a thin space where sorrow and joy meet. If you were watching me keen you would notice the change and there would be a time where you would be uncertain as to which strand I was in. As the two merge, sorrow and joy, joy prevails.

Here is the most important aspect of this work. The strand of joy is to be plucked for a longer period of time than the strand of sorrow. This strand is all about authentic joy; when it comes through me I find myself dancing in the song that flows through me. It is at this point that the transmutation process takes place so the released sorrow does not taint the worlds. Again I use Uaithne (Oo-en-ya), this ancient name of the Dagda's Harp to guide my way into being, feeling, expressing pure joy. Again, a bridge will occur between the strands of joy and peace. When peace prevails I switch from Uaithne to full on Amrun and allow the song of the Universe to be an expression of the deepest peace. I work with the song of peace to match or extend beyond the vibrational strand of joy.

In plucking the three strands this way we create space, a lightness, and freedom in our bodies. We now have more space for Spirit to move through us as hollow bones as we work Amrun into the ethers as we keen and sing home displaced and lost souls.

AMRUN

I led the group in the multi-dimensional aspects of Amrun. We sang joy through our own bodies. We worked with love, truth, freedom, beauty, and sovereignty, with the song of fire, earth, water, air, and sovereignty as we sang them into each other's bodies and into the ethers. We sang Amrun honouring the ancestors, honouring worlds between worlds and we examined our own personal as well as planetary visions in re-dreaming our lives both from an individual aspect and of Oneness.

Here is what Tara had to say after working with Amrun is such a deep way after our experiences in Jamaica:

"I am from the West Indies and it has been so meaningful for me to do this work in the West Indies. One of the biggest things that has created a special feeling within me is the working of Amrun which is the Universe speaking through us. For me it has become a way of expressing so much feeling that is inside of me that can never come through conventional words, it comes through connecting to that place that is everything and allows for such a transformation and such a depth of feeling that I have never known before — except I know it, because we are it. We just have to have the opportunity and then take it to go there. Maybe there are a million ways to say what Amrun is in different cultures and in different ways of practice. And what I know in my heart is that the more this expression comes through us, our whole experience in this world and the worlds and the dimensions and kingdoms, everything changes. To be such a conscious

part through this work makes me know that who I am is worth it, this is what I was born to do. This is what we were all born to do, we were born to be conscious in this world."

SPIRITUALITY

The way I see it is religion is exclusive whereas spirituality is inclusive.

The essence of spirituality is to offer love to self and others. This includes caring about the planet, animals, plants, as well as people. All life is sacred because of the interconnected nature of it all. The inclusiveness of Spirituality extends to a belief system whereby we are all One.

This is not a new idea. It is part of pre-Christian "Celtic" teachings, the legendary bard Aimhirghin's (OURYIN), spoke words endorsing this idea which were later scribed from oral stories by the monks. Here is an extract of what he allegedly spoke onto the wind when he first stepped onto the Emerald Isle:

I am the wind on the sea

I am the stormy wave

I am the sound of the ocean

I am the bull with seven horns

I am the hawk on the cliff face

I am the sun's tears

I am the beautiful flower

I am the boar on the rampage

I am the salmon in the pool

I am the lake on the plain…

Here is where I would like to return to the idea that I alluded to in Chapter 2. An idea that a small percentage of who I am is living in my body while the rest of me is being all of the other aspects of myself. It may seem a stretch too far for some readers yet I urge you to approach this concept with an open mind and heart.

We know that without trees we would not survive for they produce the oxygen we need to breathe as well as clearing the carbon dioxide out of the air. We know without bees there would be no pollination and therefore our food sources from the vegetable kingdom would rapidly dry up.

So it is fair to say that we are in relationship with trees and bees.

What if the mystics are right and we are all connected? What if human beings are all cells of a larger organism? What if all beings are cells of one being?

Perhaps this sounds like a utopian ideal, yet aren't the teachings of religion at heart inviting us to find space for all our brothers and sisters. Why is it that someone who looks to love, respect and appreciate all life is ridiculed as a weirdo in some sections of society? Why have we fallen so far out of alignment from love and joy?

These are questions I have asked myself all my life. It has inspired Spirit to talk through me creatively with poems and more recently songs. Here are the lyrics for a song that is based on a poem that came through me in my early twenties.

AIMHAIRGHIN

I am I am I am one

I am I am we all belong

I am a grain of corn, a windswept dune,

the golden sun, the harvest moon.

I am a blade of grass, a rose in bloom,

I'm a fertile seed, I'm the birthing womb.

I'm a dancing fire, the surging sea,

rooted in earth — sacred oak tree.

I am brother to all, I am their sister too,

Mother Father in me, is Mother Father in you.

I am I am I am one

I am I am we all belong…

ONENESS

Those who are able to buy into the concept of Oneness will understand that when we pollute the waters, we are polluting aspects of ourselves when we project hatred through thoughts and actions towards any other being we are attacking aspects of ourselves. So how do we evolve? How do we take a quantum leap into a new dimension and open up the gateways of the worlds?

CHAPTER 8: OPENING THE GATEWAYS TO THE WORLDS

TRANSMUTATION

Through transmuting the strand of sorrow into joy, we open space within our bodies for authentic joy to sing through us. We are lighter and brighter beings vibrating at a higher frequency. Take an inventory of your own bodies when you are stressed, in pain, unforgiving, angry, fatigued, and wrapped in the strand of sorrow, doesn't the life force within you feel depleted, heavy? It does in mine.

When authentic joy is coursing through my veins I feel vibrantly alive, my chest expands, as do my bodies as I breathe deeply into spaces that open up within me, I feel cleaner and my energy levels rise. Is that how it works for you? I am sure that we can agree that there is a vast difference between how the vibration of sorrow compares to the vibration of joy within us. Vibration is a key to changing the song of the Universe, vibration is a pathway that leads to both extinction and evolution. It simply depends on the frequency of our collective vibration to which tipping point we will arrive at.

Opening a vortex and singing home souls is one way to create space in the worlds for the evolutionary process to take place. This art of supporting souls who have been stuck in limbo cross over through the transmutation process is such an honour and a gift that keeps on giving. If you are still not able to comprehend this piece I am sure you will understand the difference between walking into a room where a vicious argument happened before your arrival, you may not have heard it and yet you feel the after effects still hanging in the room. There is a dark cloud, a disturbing energy left behind. However, if you enter the same room after heartfelt laughter has been bouncing off the walls, long after the jovial voices have fallen silent, the room will feel light and vibrant. There is a measurable difference. The traces of joy left in the ethers greet those who enter with glee, the anger pricks and stabs and is nauseating.

This is how sorrow and joy permeate our bodies from outside influences. We are sponges, picking up other being's vibrational songs, it is why it is important to cleanse regularly through our own transmutation rituals. Plucking the 3 Strands of Poetry is a constant in my life, a monthly practice for maintenance with daily bursts of Amrun to keep my bodies clear and healthy. Extra plucking of the strands when the sh-t hits the fan.

Why is it that I say singing home souls is a gift that keeps on giving? Every time we help a being to cross there are more beings to help support the work that we bring to the planet in the invisible realms. When we call in ancestral support we are connected to all of the beings who we have helped cross who choose to work with us for the highest good of all.

Each of us will face enormous challenges in our journeys. Many mask pain through anti-depressants and self-medication. So many souls tuning out, looking to dull their light and numb their feelings for life hurts too much to face the shadows that have consumed them. Many force a way through life with fake gloss, a pretence that allows them to get through their days. It is akin to a functioning alcoholic. They manage to hold it all together, sometimes excelling in their fields, yet behind the scenes, they are still in the clutches of disease.

There are many on the planet who feel like they have no purpose. They dislike their jobs, feel stuck in a rut and are on auto-pilot. What if we were all to wake up to a collective purpose of taking responsibility for igniting our own flames of joy?

Then there are others who walk around in a bubble of false bliss. So desperate to be in a state of joy that they ignore their own pain and suffering. Everything is "love and light" yet beneath the frozen surface of their fixed smiles is a torrent of anger, hurt, and sorrow. Each time we return to meeting ourselves, to being truthful with our own feelings and then being willing to transform the tangled threads we shift the tipping point by radiating our light authentically in the world.

Our challenge is re-patterning our thoughts and feelings so that we can plug into authentic joy to the point where we operate at a **minimum** of 51% joy to 49% sorrow. If each day, each week, each month, and each year for the next ten years we increase the percentage of joy, then perhaps, if enough us are vibrating in this way, our world will go from a wounded wasteland to a thriving realm where we all can prosper.

Finding ways to transmute sorrow into joy so peace can radiate within and without is a key to opening the gateway of the worlds. There is more than one way to activate this and for me, the 3 Strands of Poetry works. I have seen it help so many who have been introduced to it. The important thing is to find a way that works for you. There are many shamanic leaders in the world who can assist with transmutation and other healers on the planet who have techniques to support this process. Of course, it helps to talk and it is important not to get bogged down in regurgitating the problem. Finding interactive ways to release the toxins is of paramount importance. It is why we seek professionals who know how to support this process so that we refrain from splattering the strand of sorrow onto the land or projecting them onto other beings.

SINGING HOME DISPLACED/LOST SOULS

Once we have created space in our own bodies we can support the transition of lost and displaced souls. Again this practice is best served by working with someone who has expertise in this field.

The night before we were due to sing home the souls and light the 13-hour Birthing fire in Jamaica I came to the end of a book I was reading, *The Lie Tree* by Frances Hardinge.

Spirit's voice rang loud and clear in what some may still cling to as coincidence and I know to be synchronicity. I took the words she had written on the very last page of the book and the words on the very next page previewing one of her new books to circle the next morning where I shared them with the group.

They aligned perfectly with the work that was unfolding on the reef.

From *The Lie Tree*:

"I am tired of lies," said Faith. "I do not want to hide, the way Agatha did."

"So what do you want?" asked Myrtle.

"I want to help with evolution."

Spot on words that resonated through my whole being. The lies and inauthentic patterns that have permeated our world do not work. Those who work in the magical realms for the highest good of all beings are called to come out from the shadows where they have been shunned by the mainstream world and let their light shine luminously for all to see. For like Faith, I am here to help with evolution, I have faith, I am faith and I have hope that has been boosted by knowing that **We Can**!

I had sat marinating in the words from the ending of Hardinge's book in the sanctuary of the dome for some while. Waves of enthusiasm pumping through my veins with this knowing that evolution is on the horizon. It is within our capability if enough of us believe and participate in being the medicine of joy. A new tipping point is available and waiting for us to discover the New World.

I then looked at the first page of Frances' new novel *A Skinful of Shadows*. I was greeted by these words — *We See Ghosts and They Are Drawn to Us.*

"Sometimes when a person dies, their spirit goes looking for somewhere to hide. Some people have space within them, perfect for hiding."

It is why it is important to work with someone who specialises in helping souls to cross. Spirits are floating around us all of the time in a state of limbo. Learning how to be present for thousands of beings to go home is one piece, having someone who holds clear space for those who are part of this cleansing ceremony is another.

To facilitate this process, we build a Spirit Boat on the dock; we drum, rattle, row and sing Amrun as we keen the souls home, the song that sings us moves very quickly to joy. No souls are coerced to go, they are invited. We open a space for the souls to pass through as soon as the boat sets sail. This is an otherworldly journey; the Spirit Boat is guided by a person at the front who is the eyes of the boat. It was phenomenal that at the head of our boat sat a woman from the Caribbean. It was phenomenal that at the head of our boat sat a woman from the Caribbean.

Her name is Tara which means — the place of Sovereignty. It is the name of the hill in Ireland that was the place of the High King! Others on our boat were Megan, Cindy, and Margaret.

One meaning of Cindy is — Light. She sat directly behind Tara between Megan and Margaret whose names both mean — Pearl.

Behind them sat Jenn — The White Wave next to Jeff whose name means — Peaceful Pledge. Behind these two balancing the masculine and feminine were Pat — Noble and Mike — Gift from God and I stood right at the back holding space for us all drumming as Amrun flowed through my bodies into the ethers. Andrew means — Manly warrior strong and brave.

Nine souls who had all been through their own rebirthing experiences in a cave at Roaring River scrubbed and cleansed by Dr. Scott a Rasta Shaman in the rushing waters of an underground womb had prepared us well. It allowed Spirit to flow through us as water again cleansed us from the spray that lapped at the dock.

We took the boat to lands where those lost and displaced souls once originated from. We picked up other souls that were trapped in these lands and at any point, they were able to follow the light of those crossing home. Many crossed straight away and some waited until we brought the Spirit Boat back to

Jamaica, to return in a new way. As the sun kissed the earth goodnight the drumming stopped as our journey concluded, yet the vortex was left open. It remained open for the next thirteen plus hours as we moved from the dock to the fire pit and prepared for our all night celebration around the birthing fire.

We had personally cleansed our own physical, mental and spiritual bodies creating space for the birthing of new visions within us. We had helped to cleanse the planet singing home the souls with the help of the ancestors who really had our back creating space for the seeds of evolution to take root and grow.
Jackie had commented that it was typical for rain to fall on a full moon night on the reef. The clouds rolled in and it looked like rain was on the way. I went to the fire pit and spoke to Spirit and the ancestors. I have worked around all night fires before in all kinds of weather and the rain was not going to deter us. However, my words were heartfelt sharing that our commitment was to be there come what may and how wonderful it would be to honour all life under a crystal

clear star-studded sky.

I am eternally grateful to the Weather Spirits, to the assistance of all unseen beings for the sky cleared and we were held under the full light of the moon from the moment the fire was lit until the break of day.

The Brigid Flame and Dalai Lama Peace Candle burned all night long close to the small fire that carried this energy vibrantly within the licking flames. The bones of trees that had gifted their limbs were honoured in the building, tending, and fuelling of the fire. The flame was sparked at 9.53pm and the fire was fed with Amrun, rum, mugwort, juniper, oats, rose petals, and chocolate amongst other offerings including our prayers and those of the 250 people who had sent theirs in.

POWER OF PRAYER

Prior to gathering to light the fire, I had talked with the group in regards to the power of prayer. Prayer is a complete waste of time when it is a rote exercise. When we reduce prayer to mindless babble where autopilot is the order of the day we extract its life force. Prayer is fuelled on the breath when ignited and charged by passion.

Words carry power, thoughts do too, for they all have a vibration. At a lower, mumbled, automatic response that has no heart, no soul flowing through the threads, we splatter more dross into the ethers, more lethargy to weigh down the worlds. The words we choose to deliver the prayer are extremely important. What I noticed from all of the prayers sent in is that many people tangle their words and in so doing tangle their prayers.

I invited our group of nine to become cognisant of what they were praying on and how they were delivering it to the Universe. My experience of life is that the Universe loves to say yes. Sometimes we cloud our own thoughts to the point that the Universe provides a very murky manifestation that matches our jumbled thought process.

An example I gave was how some people's prayers focused on the disease, the problem, the challenge they were facing rather than the solution that would offer vibrant health and transmutation. It is indicative of how we are tangled in the strand of sorrow. It is not to say we deny our reality; however, we are looking to reweave a new way to be in the world, not to reinforce the one we are living. It also is a reflection of how challenging we find it to live in the present. What I find is many people place their prayers outside of themselves and outside of the present. A simple word used so often in prayer work — "for" — puts the prayer into the future. I believe it was Greg Braden who, many years ago, introduced me to praying "on" rather than "for" in his book the Isaiah Effect. A simple tweak shifts everything. Now instead of being in the future, the term "on" brings the prayer into the present.

Here is what Pat wrote after absorbing the information on reweaving her prayers and integrating our journey when home in the USA:

"I am continuing to enjoy my new burst of energy and all of the possibilities open to me to create more joy, freedom, and beauty in my life and on the planet. I wanted to share a major shift that occurred for me in Jamaica. You were talking about how you had to rewrite some of the prayers that were sent in because they were written within a negative framework. You gave several examples of how they could be changed. I had already written most of the prayers I wanted to put into the fire but after this discussion, I went back to reread them. Even though they were written from a place of gratitude for my prayers being answered, I realised they were written from the old paradigm and from a place of hope rather than a place of reality. This put them in the future and something still reaching for rather than in the present. When I changed the wording to express my prayers as if they were already happening EVERYTHING CAME

ALIVE. The prayers changed from an idea and hope of what could be to clear images and feelings about what is happening now and what we are moving into. I had strong visceral reactions of expansion, excitement, and joy!!! At that moment I knew for certain that I was part of the evolution of the human species and of the planet. This not only transformed my experience at the fire but has changed how I am carrying myself in the world. I now feel a deeper richness to my life, as well as being more grounded and confident about how I can participate in this extraordinary Evolution of the planet. Andrew, I thank you again for being the visionary that you are. The one to show us the way."

GUIDED BY SPIRIT

There are many visionaries stepping up to share ways of being the solution. I pray on each of us opening our hearts to hear the song that is singing through the wise ones at this time. Many young people who have stepped out of the education system because they do not see the point in working towards a future that they feel has been robbed from them because of how our generation has messed up the world. To all beings I say, "Please do not give up hope."

Yes, as a collective we may have made a royal mess of things yet there are many amongst us who have prepared ourselves to meet this challenge. Without the support of the masses, our world will reach a tipping point leading to extinction. There is time to lift our sails and boldly go where no homo sapiens have been before. Opening the gateway of the worlds is a possibility if we are willing to shed our skins and emerge from the slumber of our cocoons and fly in a (r)evolutionary way."

We can shift the tipping point through self-responsibility. By embracing solutions rather than getting tangled in the problems. By taking charge of our own personal song — the vibrational energy that we emit each day.

BLESSED BY BRIGID

I had asked the participants to head to the fire pit at 9.30pm in plenty of time for beginning our all-night celebration. I returned to the dome to make a flask of boiling water and to gather all of the offerings, the drum, the sheets of prayers, the candle, and everything else that I knew was important to be with me.

As I went to pour the water from the steaming hot kettle into my flask my hand slipped and water gushed all over my left hand. I immediately placed my hand in cool water and then realised that there was an answer on my doorstep. I gave thanks to the plant spirit of Aloe Vera and cut a piece slathering the transparent gel that is housed inside its green leaves all over my hand. Within minutes the burning sensation disappeared and the skin returned to its normal milky white colouring.

At 9.50pm I lit the candle containing the energy of the masculine and feminine — the Dalai Lama and Brigid — and handed out paper tapers to transfer the flame from the candle to the fire. I started a fire-lighting song and then added my breath to fan the flames. In so doing my head was close to the ground and my hair spilled into the flame of the candle which was beside me. My hair on the right side of my head caught alight. Two things alerted me to this, one was the gasps of some of the participants, the other was the smell. I straightened up and quickly extinguished the flame and continued fanning the fire.

Afterwards, I reflected on the blessing of water and fire on my hand and head, kissing the left feminine side and right masculine side of my body. There is a song written by Diane Baker and Anne Hill which honours Brigid and talks about blessing our hands, our heads, and our hearts. I thought about the water and the fire that creates the rainbow light and the importance of bringing our creativity to our centre, to our hearts, how my external body was blessed infusing into my physical body to bless all of the internal aspects, shooting rainbows through me to my heart. My body as a hollow bone was a microcosm of the macrocosm, a vessel of Oneness.

The heat of the water and fire were consumed instantly inside of me, no traces left behind on my skin or on my hair which looked the same the next day as it did before it was licked by the fire.

13 HOUR FIRE

I had asked people to sleep when they were no longer in the flow of Amrun, to be present with 100% and rest when not. This was adhered to and participants came and went as the hours ticked on by. I weaved thirteen rounds into the flames. Prayers were spoken in the first hour, halfway through the ceremony and then placed into a wicker person that was built where they went into the ethers as smoke, burning beautifully at the zenith of the full moon.

Spirit flowed through us. I was as energised in the last hour as I was the first hour and all of the hours that followed. We placed offerings into the sea and into the fire. The rounds of Amrun charged up the Dragon Lines fuelling our prayers and visions within the birthing fire. The rounds constituted praying on all of the elements, on sovereignty, on the balance of the feminine and masculine, on the unseen worlds, on leadership, on responsibility, on the animal, vegetable and mineral worlds, on the vibrancy of health, wellbeing and the evolution on all sentient beings.

It was a night where Spirit partied through me and those who joined the song and dance under the shining light of this Super Moon were a huge part of the celebration. I felt surges in my body as candles and fires were lit around the globe. I am so grateful to all who plugged in and joined us in the ethers. I felt your love, hope, and the beauty of your energy as you connected consciously with us.

A heron came in the betwixt and between, a bird that connects with the sun god Lugh, the visionary one in my tradition. The heron stayed throughout the morning and was still with us as we sang into the pinnacle of the full moon at 10.53am Jamaica time.

As energised as I was Spirit offered another small yet significant piece for the tapestry. After my work was completed on the reef I had two full days to rest, receive a massage, bathe in the saltwater pool, and cocoon in and around the dome before flying home to Scotland. I had my computer with me and now that I had finished my work I started to write up my experiences so I could begin to format this book. In the UK we work on 240 volts so I had a plug adaptor to charge the laptop overnight. It was then that the battery died in the computer. I noticed that overnight it had only gone up into the 80 per cent bracket rather than its full one hundred per cent. I then kept it plugged in at all times. It was the weirdest thing to work on a computer that was plugged into the mains receiving a constant charge, yet was leaking its charge by the minute rather than increasing it.

I thought about the bigger picture and the meaning behind this. What came clearly into focus is that as much energy as I have in holding space for our evolution I and those like me cannot do it alone. All of us who are working different ways to transmute sorrow into joy will continue to plug into Spirit regardless; however, without the battery — the support of the masses, we will eventually run dry, the planet will reach the tipping point of extinction and the computer — the civilisations of the world, will crash into oblivion.

Part of Tanaaz Chubb's intuitive vision that Joyce had sent to us had offered:
"This Full Moon is helping to crack us open so we can see beyond our beliefs and into a new reality."

Our wicker-person was built using one of Dr. Mike's surgical scrub shirts and a sarong of Tara's. A balance of the feminine and masculine. Of Sovereignty — the Goddess (Tara) and a Gift from God (Mike). Interestingly the scrub shirt and sarong are worn by both genders in the world!

As the wicker-person met the flames I handed my fire tending stick to Tara and both she Mike worked with this sacred offering. The bundle of prayers was tucked into its heart space. The two of them made sure the flames from the wicker-person stayed within the boundary of the fire pit. With so many pages of prayers, assistance was required for the bundle of prayers to ignite. We watched as they literally prised open the heart — cracking open the prayers and visions so we can birth a way to see beyond our beliefs and into a new reality.

At this exact moment, three dolphins surfaced off of the reef. I saw the symbolism here of communication, playfulness, resurrection, joy, protection, cooperation, gentleness, peace, wisdom and balance. The fact that there were three brought my understanding of how these attributes were glowing in the rebirthing of the physical, mental, and spiritual bodies within all beings.

Megan brought her guitar down to the fire and before we went for a luxurious breakfast feast of fresh fruit and ackee we wailed joyfully into the ethers singing Bob Marley's Redemption Song.

CHAPTER 9: JOINING THE EVOLUTION

CRACKED OPEN

Tanaaz's intuitive insights proved true in that we had all been cracked open — I had transitioned from hope to knowing. A small shift and yet poignant for everything has changed because of it. Each of us that had gathered around the fire felt the shifts. Jackie's staff team felt the shifts. Stephanie, the Yoga teacher, came the following day and remarked how visceral her experience was the moment she lit a candle and connected with the fire from her home near Negril.

A retreat such as this will always bring things up for in working these ways we meet ourselves. I have always maintained that working in the wild climes of nature there is nowhere to hide. The land is authentic — it naturally invites us to meet ourselves when we spend time with the elements. We either run away from our fears or we face them and step through them. It is not an easy place to be and quite often it is an uncomfortable place to be.

Mike Fenster was challenged to put a voice to an experience that on the outset scared the crap out of him and once he had the chance to sit with it and to voice it to me prior to singing home the lost and displaced souls, he found his horizon had shifted to meet him in a truly magical way. Interestingly, the sound that he heard was one that also caught my attention. I had risen twice out of bed to check out the drumming and cries that were on the wind. When I arose a third time it was after sleep and it was when the image of Christopher Columbus and the vision of truly weaving a new world transpired.

Here are Mike's words to describe his vision that he witnessed off of the reef that night that prized him open in a huge way.

DR. MIKE'S WORDS

"Hospitals smell of death, especially in the winter.

But it was not that smell, too familiar, that brought me there that evening. Nor was it any number of tropical scents carried on the tidal winds in the rising darkness.
It was the sound. A deep rhythmic fury emanating from the ocean herself. A thunderous repeating fractal of a chant; off key and off rhythm yet entraining, nonetheless. It has left me a story to share before I pass along.

I walked into the deep of night and sat at the waters' edge. The clouds came, and parted, and came again. They brought transient mists, cloaking me in cool dampness between the shadow and the light. And still, the sea bellowed a hauntingly familiar, but yet undecipherable refrain.

*The sea mist rolled in and settled upon the reefs
offshore, backlit from some ethereal cathedral in the
distance. The air grew heavier and at the same time,
the mists that had encroached upon the island drew
back their curtains. Stretched from horizon to horizon
was an endless armada of ancient tall ships. Small
bright points of light buzzed about them like swarms of
fireflies upon a summer meadow's eve. The very vital
essence seemed to be sucked out of the air. There was
simply no denying; this was a flotilla of the dead.*

*The overwhelming emotion that accompanies Death,
magnified by the presence of so many, washed upon
the shores. With each breaking wave, my eyes looked
for a longboat and crew, come to shanghai me across
the breakers. Even with that dread apprehension, I
was rooted to my seat upon the rocks. Glued with
incredulity of the sheer spectacle of it all, I watched
and felt the otherworldly presence. I slowly drowned
on dry land even as the dark sky shuddered with the
cracking of dawn; lightening with milky promise as
everything night bound receded.*

Although no ferryman had come to call my passage, they might as well have. The next day found me drained, soul-sucked. I was physically present, spiritually depleted, and mentally numb with my rationality throwing a temper tantrum like a three year stomping about simply screaming, "No, no, no."

It took the entire day to get words around the event so an inner dialogue could list, categorize and accept, if not entirely explain, the preceding night's events. About then, of course, we jumped into the vortex. Aligned at the water's edge once again, this time with the setting sun, I joined the crew. We were here for those dead, or perhaps more accurately they had come not for us, but because of us.

Andrew beat the drum, the chants began, and ships once again appeared off the edges of the horizon and ordinary reality. A fusillade of bright orbs manifested before us. They traveled hither and thither, many working their way slowly to my left. Some rose from the very waters; some dove back into the deep. Others soared high into the sky; still, others hovered about like non-committal observers of some mundane sidewalk sideshow. One large orb locked into eye level. An intensity of power was clearly present as it scanned, coming closer and brighter. Then as if with a careless grin it shot high into the sky seeming as if it would leave the earth and blast into orbit. Then, with equal fervor, it plunged straight down into the deep ocean and was gone.

We continued the process as the sun reached its nadir on the horizon, and the orbs became fewer. A pleasant catharsis took hold as Evening put her hand on our shoulder for a job well-done. To dance with the dead and sing with the gods; to glory in magic and self, and paint the universe with our thoughts- these are the days we live for and in turn, these are the days that give us a life of authentic purpose."

Mike voiced his own paradigm shift after the completion of our work together stating,

"I had the unique privilege of being here in Jamaica with Andrew Steed and once again all my pre-conceived notions, expectations, dreams, desires were shattered in a positive way and hopefully I leave a better person, no let me correct that, I know I leave a better person from being here. This was a very transformative, powerful and interesting week. It was even more than medicine, it provided a way, I leave with a sense of a way of being that is now as intertwined as any strand of DNA in my cells, in my body. And perhaps this is the DNA that links our physical body and cells and organs with our spirit and soul. As a heart Doctor, I place a lot of emphasis obviously on the importance and singular uniqueness of cardiovascular function in maintaining our physical bodies. I was blown away how Andrew Steed is a master spiritual cardiologist. Really for me the transition from the appreciation of the magnificent physical function of the heart to what it means to our

spirit, to work our dreams, our destinies through our
spiritual heart. As anyone can see who turns on the
news for five minutes the world is calling for a whole
lot more spiritual heart, as any patient who is in
urgent need of a stent in their left anterior descending
artery, so I would say leaders like Andrew are not only
spiritual cardiologists, they are interventional spiritual
cardiologists and I was one of those people who
needed an intervention."

JOINING THE EVOLUTION

So I ask, "Won't you help to sing this song of
Amrun?" It is time for the sound healers to step
forward, the joyous ones whose hearts vibrate
authentically with the power of love. As we raise the
vibration of our own bodies, we create space for the
vibration to resonate at a higher frequency. In so
doing, we have an opportunity to crack open hidden
spaces where the power of evolution lives awaiting the
discovery of the richest treasure we have ever known.
An opening of consciousness, an opening of the
gateways to the worlds.

Yet, please remember to transmute the strand of sorrow to joy so we don't just paint over the cracks. Let's vibrate authentically and change the trajectory of hopelessness and extinction to knowing and evolution!

VIBRATION

I am no scientist and yet I understand that we live in a Universe where all physical bodies are made up of matter. This includes galaxies, stars, planets, rocks, water, air, plants, animals, and humans.

If I understand things correctly all matter, everything in the Universe is energy and all energy exists at a different level of vibration. The Universe is in perpetual motion — it is one huge vibration.

Is it so hard to imagine that we are part of this universal song? A vibrational energy that is connected to something far greater and far bigger than ourselves? Are you able to open your imagination to being a melody of this song, this symphony, this musical expression of oneness?

Science tells us that our thoughts are energy and they vibrate.

Is all of this starting to come together for you? The Universe is vibrating at the level that we co-create. Our thoughts, our actions throughout the history of the planet are vibrating in the ethers. It is crystal clear we have globally placed a greater emphasis on plucking the strand of sorrow rather than the strand of joy since time immemorial.

As you are aware, this strand includes all of the aspects that I have labelled under the banner of sorrow. Of course, there is authentic joy and peace that are part of our world yet our planet is sick because we are sick.

We have vibrated all aspects of our diseases and unprocessed deaths into all of the nooks and crannies of our world over eons. We have created a congested heavy and chaotic world where there is a distinct lack of space. The planet has been fed by jagged vibrations of a very low frequency over an extended period of time which is rapidly leading us towards a tipping point.

What science tells us in our thoughts matter, they go into the ethers as vibrations of energy. Who is in charge of your thoughts? Who do you speak to more than anyone else on the planet? If you are like me, then it is yourself. What are we saying to ourselves?

What I found liberating in Joyce's message sharing Tanaaz' words with me was that we're on point. We were looking to be the solution rather than the problem. We created space in our bodies and through sound, thought, and movement we remembered ourselves under this rebirthing moon. We birthed space into our bodies so we could hold more space for others in this world. We created space for more ancestral support through singing home the souls.

I do not have all of the answers to what the evolution will look like; what I do have is a pathway to help us get there. What if by creating space we open up gateways within ourselves that allow us to evolve physically, mentally, and spiritually? What if we tapped into the inner sanctum of our souls in Universal Oneness?

What I do know is that by creating authentic joy within us and around us we will co-create a more peaceful world.

YOGA

Each morning on the reef, we arose to Yoga before breakfast. It was not compulsory and I strongly recommended it to our group. As I have stated many times, our journey of the retreat was to create space within our bodies, the Yoga instructor offered us the opportunity to stretch all of our bodies, with exercise and a morning visualisation. I was particularly pleased to meet Stephanie Oretzki, our instructor, as she was open to working with what I had planned for the group each day. She designed the morning class to meet us where we were at on the day of release, the day of visioning, the day of rebirth and she provided a wonderful space for activating energy in our physical, mental, and spiritual bodies. She also added a list of prayers to be placed in the all-night fire.

Stretching our body after a night's sleep is so invigorating. Moving helps to release blocks of tension, stress and assisted by all of the shamanic work, it supported the expansion of space in us all.

It is in all the little shifts that we make major shifts. I wonder how many of us take time to stretch and work out our bodies each day? There are so many ways to do this, it is finding what works best for us and then creating space to physically, mentally, and spiritually committing to stretch out each day.

FOOD

Dr. Mike Fenster has written several excellent books on our relationship with food and he, like all of us, marvelled at the culinary delights that were served to us each morning and evening by Gwen and Vanetta the two chefs at the retreat centre who were aided by Nick and at times Jackie.

Jackie grows a lot of produce in her own gardens, everything else is locally resourced, organic and of the highest quality.

It is so important when working with energy in such a deep way that we nurture and nourish our bodies. I am thankful to Jackie and her staff team for the exceptional job that they do in holding us in such beautiful ways. What we put into our bodies on a daily basis fuels us. The question to ask ourselves is what quality fuel are we using to carry our vehicles to meet each moment of our lives? How well are we maintaining our vehicle? Where are we resourcing our foods from? What footprint are we leaving on the planet? How have beings been treated in giving their lives so that way may live? Are we ingesting traumatised foods, polluted with fear, chemicals, growth hormones, pesticides, and/or ingredients that are depleting the wellbeing of the planet?

I advocate the importance of our life choices outside of retreats. If we only eat well when we go to a wellness retreat, if we only receive a massage then and stretch our bodies with some form of physical exercise in these moments, we are not able to operate at maximum efficiency on a daily basis. This is not rocket science and yet so many people on the planet have poor diets and are unfit.

CONSCIOUS LIVING

Keeping ourselves in shape, creating space in our own homes, both our body temple and the abode where we rest our head each night, are all a part of supporting a healthy lifestyle. Everything matters, the cleaning agents we use, the companies we support through our purchases, our recycling efforts, our whole life choices matter.

I know that I fall down in being in sovereignty with the land. For starters I drive a car that is fuelled by diesel, I fly on planes regularly as my work takes me around the globe. These two acts right here go against supporting the planet breathing. It means that I look to make an extra effort in other areas of my life and to be more conscious of my footprint on the planet.

I address the pollution that my travels cause by working even more diligently with Amrun into the ethers, through the prayers and healing energy that I offer to the planet, and by looking to spread more authentic joy through all of my interactions with others. We have all heard the phrase "treat others how you wish to be treated." For those of us who readily accept the idea of Oneness, those others that we are either treating well or poorly are ourselves anyway!

When we add a sparkle to someone else's day don't we feel more radiant for it? I know I do. What if each of us took a step towards seeing ourselves more clearly and in so doing recognising that you and I are One.

Conscious living requires us to be present with ourselves and each moment. During the retreat, everything was heightened and in some ways, it is much easier to be present when we are outside the mundane aspects of our lives. Yet life is all about bringing magic into the mundane. When we embrace the mundane tasks of life in a magical way albeit washing dishes, cleaning the toilet, shopping for groceries or standing in a queue, we place a very different energy into the ethers than when we are on auto-pilot or in despair as we try and get through it all.

WAKING UP

Of course, waking up and living more consciously requires effort and change on our part. What if each of us actively monitors the carbon footprint we are leaving on the planet and then commits to reducing it? Right here we will make a difference.

Joyce and I know we still leave a large trace on the planet with our car, air travel and the utilities we use in this modern world, yet we have drastically scaled back and have become far more conscious of the way we live. It doesn't mean that we can't do more, we can. We have reduced the products we use that have palm oil within them, we purchase less stuff, we are conscious of packaging, we are vegetarians, we use less plastic and still we leave a footprint. I have included a short section in regards to palm oil in the resources section of the book.

Joyce is phenomenal at researching products that support the wellbeing of the planet. We are far from perfect and we are challenging ourselves to better guardians of the planet than we have ever been. It has meant making sacrifices including giving up some of our favourite brands of chocolate. We still have palm oil in our toothpaste though the brand we use is one of the kindest to the planet and only uses sustainable palm oil, even this will change as Joyce is currently embarking on making our own toothpaste. We only fly to lead gatherings no longer for personal pleasure and those who fly to us are involved in actively working a medicine way to transmute sorrow to joy in a variety of ways both for personal and planetary healing.

Would I let go of all of this and live car and travel free in my village? Yes, I would in a heartbeat if we lived in a community whereby I could offer my services as a medicine person and have the local community provide food and accommodation for doing so. This as yet is not happening, so like Greta Thunberg who is travelling the world to raise awareness, I will continue to go where Spirit calls to work with groups and bring more people to the fires of change.

VISION

I felt a monumental difference in having 250 people's prayers to add to the birthing fire and their active participation through the ethers. What if we raised that number exponentially? I have more full moon fires planned for 2019, 2020 and beyond. I will be inviting prayers to be sent into me. I also have a vision of other shamanic leaders and healers throughout the world building small full moon fires and bringing large communities together along with opening up these gatherings to extended communities who send in their prayers to them. We can then connect all of our fires/candles together, we can sing to each other as we sing through the Dragon Lines and 250 prayers can multiple to 250 million! Why not? We have to start somewhere, we can build this pathway to evolution, we have it in us, we are magical stardust, we are one!

FOLLOW UP

My hope is that you have reached this segment in the book and you are called to get aboard this boat, this ship and sail into a new tipping point. To help us get there I am going to be leading a series of cost-effective gatherings online to discuss this work and interactively share Amrun, the 3 Strands of Poetry, and the Gateway to Change in more detail. My intending is to help us all build muscle to be active participants in a journey that steers us away from extinction into the realms of evolution.

If you are a leader in your community called to connect your fire with mine, please be in touch. If you are a seeker who is called to join the evolution, please be in touch. If this book has touched your heart in any way, please buy copies for friends and family. I have kept the costs low for a reason, to make it affordable to gift multiple copies albeit on audio, e-book or hardcopy. Let's spread the word that "WE CAN" my prayers are that we invoke the brother and sister of "WE CAN" — "WE WILL" and "WE WILL DO IT/BE IT RIGHT NOW!"

For

We are Children of the Evolution!

RAW

RESOURCES

www.andrewsteed.com

Other Books by the author Andrew Steed available on Amazon:

Magical Crows Ravens and the Celebration of Death
Magical Elephants and the True Meaning of Strength
13 Steps to Bringing Magic into Your Life
Powering Up Our Life Stories
The First Santa

Sacred Outcast — A CD of Spirit Songs available on I-Tunes, Amazon and CD Baby.

INTUITIVE ASTROLOGER
Tanaaz Chubb — www.foreverconscious.com

FRONT COVER ARTIST
Jayde Hilliard — www.jaydehilliard.com

Dr. Michael Fenster — www.chefdrmike.com

Jackies on the Reef — www.jackiesonthereef.com

PALM OIL

Why is palm oil such a problem? If you are not aware of the devastation that is caused by our daily usage of palm oil, then this will be an eye-opener for you. If you are, then like Joyce and I, we hope that you are already taking active steps to reduce the products that you purchase that contain them.

Palm oil production is and has been responsible for human rights violations, through the forced removal of Indigenous Peoples and rural communities from land that is required for the expansion of palm oil plantations. Add to this the issues of child labour abuse and modern day slavery and you begin to get a glimpse into why it is important to wake up to the atrocities that are happening around the globe.

Deforestation on a wide scale basis has seriously impacted the well-being of the planet. With the clearing of rainforests comes significant carbon pollution which is a major contributor to climate change. Add to this the cost of innocent lives that have been swept aside to stock grocery stores full of products for general purchase. Countless trees whose ancestral roots have graced this earth have been ripped up and hacked down. The knock on effect of obliterating one of the planet's most diverse ecosystems is to the detriment of its inhabitants. Wildlife such as the Sumatran Rhino, Sumatran Elephant, and the Sumatran and Bornean Orangutan are on the verge of extinction.

Things shift fast on the planet and just when you think you have found a product that is free from the strings of the companies embroiled in practices that are plucking the strand of sorrow most keenly, they are bought out an amalgamated into these corporations.

Joyce spends hours researching companies looking for ethical practices. Here is a list of a few products that you may have put in your basket for check out in the last week that could well contain palm oil: Chocolate, bread, margarine, ice cream, soap, toothpaste, shampoo, detergent, pizza, crisps, lipstick, biscuits/cookies.

And just because it doesn't list palm oil as an ingredient doesn't mean it does not contain it. According to the WWF, World Wild Fund, the derivatives of palm oil can appear under more than twenty other names!

Being conscious takes effort. There is no easy "quick fix" way to know which companies are legitimately honouring an agreement made at the UN Climate summit in 2014 to cut deforestation by half with a view to ending it by 2030.

Thanks to worldwide pressure from individuals, scientists, and organisations such as Amnesty International, Rainforest Action Network, WWF and Greenpeace, things have shifted in the last decade. It is important for us lay people to wake up and have the vision to be responsible for reading labels and researching what we feed our bodies and where it comes from.

We are the people we have been waiting for. Your choices, my choices, our choices matter!

Printed in Great Britain
by Amazon